MW01181196

PRAISE FOR TEACHING KIDS TO BE GOOD PEOPLE

"Stellar! Unlike many solution-based parenting books, *Teaching Kids to Be Good People* is insightful, intuitive on so many levels . . . a truly meaningful book for our times. In an era when we feel confused about how to stay connected with our teens, Annie gives us practical, *new* advice we can use right now! The stories are so well written, you won't want to get up, so grab a cup of Joe in a comfy chair and turn off your phone. This book is going to change your relationships!"
—Lynne Kenney, Psy.D., author of *The Family Coach Method*

"Annie Fox's experience as an educator, parent and educator of parents shows in her new book *Teaching Kids to Be Good People*. Her learning-by-doing lessons and, actually, in every

sentence of this wonderful, readable, friendly book about how to (with a little luck) turn all people into friends—especially friends of the most at risk people—teenagers."
—Rick Ackerly, author of *The Genius in Every Child: Encouraging Character, Curiosity, and Creativity in Children*

"I wholeheartedly recommend *Teaching Kids to Be Good People* to any significant adult in children's lives. This book offers guidance and practical advice to ensure that children are supported to become the best that they can be. The best not only for themselves, but the best also for their families, schools, communities, and the world!"
—Sue McNamara, Director of Education
Six Seconds South East Asia

"Annie Fox has a genuine passion for helping our young people and she has many years of experience doing it. Both are evident in this wonderful resource for parents and teachers. It's full of insight, wisdom, good stories, and most important—practical advice. I highly recommend it for anyone wanting to help our kids become good people."
—Dr. Hal Urban, Ed.D., author of
Life's Greatest Lessons and *20 Gifts of Life*

"Timing is everything, and the time has come for this book! *Teaching Kids to Be Good People* not only helps parents introduce and support their children's emotions, it also reminds adults that we too must honor and release our deeply held feelings as well. The time has come!"
—Sharon Silver, CPE, author of *Stop Reacting and Start Responding: 108 Ways to Discipline Consciously and Become the Parent You Want to Be*

"Annie has been helping teens use their moral compass and parents and educators to support young people's development of one for 30 years, and her very readable latest book—*Teaching Kids to Be Good People*—has that level of experience, plus wisdom, anecdotes, exercises, and compass-development tools packed into it. I highly recommend this book. In it, Annie connects 21st century parenting to the wisdom of the ages."

—Anne Collier, journalist, youth advocate and co-director of ConnectSafely.org

"Having worked in this field for so long, it becomes increasingly difficult to read new thoughts and ideas. Every time I read something of Annie's, it makes me think. Great book; a great job Annie!"

—Sarah Newton, author of *Help! My Teenager Is an Alien!*

"Raising happy, confident, emotionally intelligent, compassionate kids is not always easy in these 24/7 digitally online times. Finding positive, empathetic role models is often difficult, but *Teaching Kids to Be Good People*, a wonderfully practical and warm-hearted book, is a great place to start. It will empower parents with some really helpful suggestions and ideas for navigating the choppy emotional waters of raising great adults. I highly recommend that you settle down with a cup of coffee and enjoy reading *Teaching Kids to Be Good People* as Annie's ideas will make communicating with your children meaningful and magical."

—Sue Atkins, author of *Parenting Made Easy—How to Raise Happy Children*

"Another work of magic from what I have come to know as a master in the field. Sharing actual scenarios and follow up questions helps to keep readers connected to Annie's ideas in a way that most parenting books fail to do."

—Joe Bruzzese, M.A., founder of Sprigeo.com, author of *A Parents' Guide to the Middle School Years*

"I love it: it is full of practical advice, much of which I have yet to read elsewhere. We are already implementing Annie's approach to some issues with our own three young monkeys. We can foresee Annie's book as a guide as we enter the tween years and beyond."

—Dr. Russell A. Faust, Ph.D., M.D.,
founder of Ask the Booger Doctor

"*Teaching Kids to Be Good People* is a step-by-step template for parents who want to help their kids and themselves survive and thrive through the challenges of parenthood. In an age where many parents want to be their child's best friend and often lose sight of the need for actively using parenting skills, I commend Ms. Fox for writing such a clear parenting guide and thank her for being 'just in time.' This book also should find its way on to the office shelves of school counselors and school psychologists."

—Louise Sattler, NCSP, founder of Signing Families™

"Annie Fox's *Teaching Kids to Be Good People* is an insightful work that looks to understand the minds of the younger generation and how we can all work together to make this world a better and safer place to live. When I first started to read I had my doubts. How can a book teach parents how to better educate their children without sounding too condescending? But I was hooked as Fox provides an interactive experience, continuously engaging readers in the conversation while showing that she, too, is not perfect, and we are all constantly learning how to better improve ourselves so that we may be good role models."

—Mackenzie Gavel, blogger, founder of Belittle The Bullies

"*Teaching Kids to Be Good People* delivers a thought-provoking and stimulating read. Annie Fox stands as a parent-educator and author bringing the importance of character education to the forefront of parenting issues."

—Denise Murray, Educational Consultant,
Creative Learning Center

TEACHING KIDS
TO BE
GOOD PEOPLE

OTHER BOOKS BY ANNIE FOX

☞ The Teen Survival Guide to Dating and Relating

☞ Too Stressed to Think? A Teen Guide to Staying Sane When Life Makes You Crazy (with Ruth Kirschner)

☞ Middle School Confidential Book 1: Be Confident in Who You Are

☞ Middle School Confidential Book 2: Real Friends vs. the Other Kind

☞ Middle School Confidential Book 3: What's Up with My Family?

☞ Are You My Friend? A Raymond and Sheila Story

☞ Are We Lost? A Raymond and Sheila Story (2013)

More at Books.AnnieFox.com

TEACHING KIDS TO BE GOOD PEOPLE

PROGRESSIVE PARENTING

FOR THE 21ST CENTURY

BY ANNIE FOX, M.ED.

Published by
Electric Eggplant
www.ElectricEggplant.com
+1 (415) 534-5437
press@ElectricEggplant.com

Copyright © 2012 by Annie Fox. All rights reserved.

Edited by Douglas Fehlen
Cover and interior design by Daniel Will-Harris

ISBN-13: 978-1480083936
ISBN-10: 1480083933

Visit us at
TeachingKidsToBeGoodPeople.com

DEDICATION

To David, who makes it all possible

CONTENTS

INTRODUCTION

Obviously not all teachers are parents,
but all parents are teachers.

That's convenient because good character traits, like empathy and respect, are teachable skills that need to be learned at home as well as at school. When we teach kids to be good people we help the world become a safer, saner, more equitable place for all of us. Nothing is more important than that!

But these are tough times for character educators. I know because I've been working in schools with students, teachers, and parents for more than 30 years as well as online since 1997. The job is getting harder. The values promoted by mass media work against us. What passes for entertainment is frequently mean-spirited. Character assassination in public discourse is the air we breathe, and the resulting pollution is a hazard to our well-being. It's a huge problem, but what can we do?

When our kids plug in, which is most of the time, they encounter few positive adult role models. Online and off, our culture frequently ignores or rewards cruelty. This is why our children desperately need us to do a better job mentoring them in the direction of respect and kindness.

Our kids are good kids, but they are constantly challenged by the less-than-compassionate standards of their peers with whom they are mind-linked 24/7. Today's teens suffer from status anxiety at levels no other generation has endured. This compels them to do whatever it takes to fit in, including things they are not particularly proud of. Despite these ubiquitous challenges I am confident we can teach our kids to be good people who actively seek opportunities to help others and who have the social courage to act on their good intentions.

We parent-educators are gardeners. We plant seeds and offer nurturing lessons that our kids can internalize. But we are not our children's only influencers. By rededicating ourselves to teaching our kids to be good people, we provide them with the tools to do the right thing while we're right there beside them and when they're on their own. Whether they actually do it, is *their* choice. But at least we'll know we've done our part well.

To help on our parenting journey, I've written this very personal and pragmatic guide that includes essays, podcasts, prompts, tools, questions, answers, and self-assessment quizzes all for the purpose of teaching kids to be good people.

How do you define a "good person?" That's what I wanted to find out, so I crowdsourced the answer by posting the question. I received hundreds of responses. Eight concepts kept reappearing: Emotional intelligence, ethics, help, forgiveness, compassion, empathy, acceptance, and social courage—all essential, teachable skills. This book will help you teach them to your children or students. Hopefully, we'll become so engaged in this process that we will inspire all of our children to become part of the solution.

So much of me

Is made of what I learned from you

You'll be with me

Like a handprint on my heart.

Because I knew you,

I have been changed . . . for good.

  —Stephen Schwartz, WICKED

1: HOW DO YOU FEEL? NO, REALLY.

LEARNING TO MANAGE EMOTIONS

"If your emotional abilities aren't in hand, if you don't have self-awareness, if you are not able to manage your distressing emotions, if you can't have empathy and have effective relationships, then no matter how smart you are, you are not going to get very far."

—Daniel Goleman, *Emotional Intelligence*

One of the hardest skills to master, aside from parallel parking, is staying cool in the face of destructive emotions—our own or someone else's. It's incredibly tough because jealousy, contempt, rage, and all their cousins just show up to the party, uninvited. Even if we got the memo, our brain is not designed to hold back from feeling what we feel. A situation, a word, a look, even a thought can ignite a fuse, and when the bomb of destructive impulses explodes, we're held hostage, from the inside. At those moments it's a challenge for adults to keep our behavior in check. For kids, it can be nearly impossible, unless we talk to them, listen to them, and teach them that all feelings are valid, but not even the hottest hate gives us a free pass to hurt anyone. That's why teaching kids to be good people, involves helping them to understand emotions so they can learn to diffuse their own incendiary devices before losing control and hurting someone.

A LITTLE BREAKFAST AND A BIG LESSON IN EMOTIONAL INTELLIGENCE

My mother's sobs woke me. Behind the door of my parents' bedroom, I heard my father comforting her. My brothers told me that Grandpa had *died*. My five-year-old brain wasn't sure what to make of that, so I stood paralyzed in the darkened hallway, not knowing how I was supposed to feel. Suddenly Mommy opened her door, her wavy hair freshly brushed, her lipstick bright red. She smiled and cheerfully asked what I wanted for breakfast. I wasn't hungry. I was confused. I had a lot of questions. I needed to be comforted, but Mommy's tight smile warned me to be "good." So I said nothing.

Later, as I pushed a piece of French toast around my plate, I had a realization—an absolute epiphany: *Grownups hide their sadness!*

When I was 15 my father died of a massive heart attack. His sudden passing left a huge hole in my heart, but instead of grieving, I decided that since I was now all grown up I had to suppress my sadness.

Fast-forward 25 years. My dentist, replacing a cracked filling from childhood, pauses, asks how I'm doing and gently rests a hand on my head. A tidal wave of sadness overwhelms me. I start weeping and cannot stop.

For the next 48 hours I'm emotionally numb and clueless about what the hell is happening. My husband, David, helps me realize that the dentist's touch reminded me of my father and the way he often tousled my hair. With that revelation, the floodgates burst. Finally I am able to grieve for my dad and release myself from feelings that held me hostage for decades.

That day I learned what really happens when we leave intense emotions unexpressed. They don't actually "fade away," as I had believed. Instead, they work like a mild acid, slowly eroding our insides, boring holes in our emotional foundation, creating gaps in our ability to be ourselves and fearlessly open up to others.

When I finally unwrapped that life-lesson, I was done burying feelings that needed to be expressed. I vowed to teach my children, through my own example, how to express emotions in healthy ways. As the universe is always eager to help us fill the gaps in our education, I soon got my big chance to "walk the walk." Actually, I ended up running.

During most of 1994 my mom was dying of Lou Gehrig's Disease. Every day I drove an hour each way to see her. During continuous *Scrabble* tournaments, Mom and I finally found the words to communicate with an intimacy we'd never shared before. I am eternally grateful for those last ten months we had together . . . grace-filled and excruciatingly painful as they were.

After spending each day with Mom, I arrived home, scared, worn down, and so raw. I offered no one a lipstick smile. Instead, I trusted that David, our daughter, and son (then ages 15 and 9) would know how to respond to a person in need. Their back rubs, cups of tea, and loving words of encouragement got me through that endless year. If I'd chosen the charade of "Everything's fine, honey. What would you like to eat?" I'd have betrayed myself and robbed my children of an opportunity to learn what it means to be a *mensch, aka* a real human being. By displaying the truth of my vulnerability, I offered the kids a golden opportunity to show compassion (toward me and their grandmother) and to grow beautifully toward adulthood. They took what they were given and raced off with it, farther than I ever would have imagined.

REAL WORLD ASSIGNMENT:
Emotional Intelligence (EQ) Legacy

We take away life lessons from the parenting we receive. Awareness of our own EQ legacy from childhood can inspire the personal changes needed to create healthier relationships with other adults and with our own children.

Fuel for Thought—While you were growing up, how challenging was it for you to express emotions? Was it fairly easy for you to talk about how you felt, or was yours a family that typically "swept things under the rug?" Could you freely express anger to your parents? Worry? Hurt? Love? If you don't remember what it was like and you've got a sibling, check in with him/her and compare notes.

Conversations That Count—Discuss with your child the communication challenges you faced growing up. Find a way to talk that's honest and still respectful of your parents or their memory. Even if you had no major obstacles with your parents, there's always room for improvement. Ask your child: "How can I do a better job being the kind of parent who is easy to talk to? How could *you* do a better job letting me know what you need when you're upset or worried?" Talk with an open heart. Listen with an open mind.

NOTE: Throughout this book you'll find guided discussions meant for you and your child, *aka* Conversations That Count. For them to really count, make it safe for your child to be real with you. Model respectful listening. If your child says something you're not thrilled to hear, calm down before responding. (Slow deep breaths are infinitely useful parenting tools.) Getting defensive, contradicting your child's words, and invalidating what's being said are all quick ways to shut down a conversation. Communication flows more effectively when we listen to each other with respect and show that we are trying to understand the other person's perspective (even when disagreeing). We all want to be heard and understood. Model that.

Teach—Use at least one insight gained from your conversation to make it safer to express feelings in your family. We're not looking for perfection, just progress toward better communication and a closer bond with people we love. When we lose control of our emotions or lose sight of our teaching objectives, we need to apologize and put real effort into doing a better job next time. The way we express and respond to emotions teaches our children so much about being part of a healthy family and being a real friend. Down the road, what they learn from us will also make them more compassionate partners and parents.

WHAT WOULD YOU TEACH HERE?

*My eight-year-old stepson is a sweet kid. We love each other and I try to be a good stepdad. He's been diagnosed with **ADHD**. I get upset having a child running my life, telling me what to do, pushing every boundary he can and making my wife and I miserable because he doesn't always get his way. I feel like the outcast sometimes. I haven't talked to my wife yet about how I'm feeling. —My child's teacher*

Read my reply (AA 1.1)

HALLOWEEN AND THE ART OF FAKING IT

I love Halloween. Always have. Even though our kids don't live here any more, David and I still trawl the neighborhood, checking out trick-or-treaters and home makeovers. David usually wears his multimedia producer costume— understated, but totally convincing. Typically I pull out all the stops and morph into a mime with whiteface, red-bow lips, massive amounts of black eyeliner, and a pink tutu on my head.

My senior year in high school I was voted Class Actress, so I fully appreciate the fascination with taking on a new persona and milking it for all it's worth. The irony isn't lost on me that this great pretender has built a career exploring the MO of kids who constantly fake it by pretending to be someone they're not, just to get other kids to like them.

I recently emailed a bunch of middle and high school students and asked: "How do you know when you're faking it?" Here are some answers:

☞ "I have a feeling of guilt and hatred for myself. I feel like I'm a wimp for not speaking the truth."

☞ "It's hard for me to really shine through and show people who I am because I am always worried about impressing them. I hate it when I act this way."

☞ "I feel like a fraud in my own body. I feel betrayed by myself because I'm not showing everyone who I am and it hurts because I don't know if they will like me for who I am."

☞ "I get a nagging feeling tugging at the back of my brain, telling me 'Don't do this, you know this isn't you.'"

☞ "Whenever I'm putting on 'my mask' I feel sort of terrible and messy inside, like a lot of spaghetti, all tangled up. I feel almost sick to my stomach and a little anxious, but I still do it to impress others. But it never feels quite right. I do it because I feel like I'm not good enough sometimes."

Their responses saddened me. We want our kids to be happy and self-assured. We want them to be courageous enough to drop the mask and confidently be themselves. But that's a huge challenge when they're unwilling to make a move without first checking out what everyone else is doing. If everyone else is being unkind, our children need tremendous strength of character not to join the hating party. Because the price of social poker is so very high, not many of them are willing to gamble.

Of course some kids embrace their authentic self and don't hesitate to do the right thing. They show their goodness with equal confidence when no one is watching and when *everyone* is watching. But more kids need that kind of courage. Too many teens are Peer Approval Addicts, compulsively doing whatever it takes to fit in, including stuff they're not proud of. For them, everyday is Halloween, only they don't get candy—just the hollow feeling of wimping out and not being "good enough" without their mask.

How can we help our kids resist conforming to negative peer behavior? By modeling and reinforcing, early and often, what authenticity looks like. By teaching that our choices matter and everyone deserves respect even when we're feeling angry with them. Let's talk about people in the news, characters in books, movies, TV shows, and anyone we know did the right thing despite the risk that friends might not approve. Let our sons and daughters know that they already are "enough" of everything that matters. Remind them that they've got the courage to do the right thing, even when they're not sure they do.

A week after my first survey question, I followed up with this one: "How would your life be different if you didn't have to worry what other people think?" Here's what they said:

☞ "I'd probably share with people that 'Hey, being yourself is cool, and if you can't do this now . . . why not?'"

☞ "I would not spend a lot of money or do stupid things just to fit in."

☞ "I would try out for football with the boys."

☞ "I'd go to school in costume every day, dressed as a medieval knight, an astronaut, a soldier, or something totally new!"

☞ "I wouldn't formulate the perfect words to say to those perfect people. I would say exactly how I feel."

☞ "I would eat a cheesecake and wear a flannel vest. Whoa! That would be a pretty darn cool world!"

☞ "I would love it! It would be like a freedom that lets you *fly*."

I've got no guaranteed tip sheet for you at this point, just a simple question: As a parent, what could you do, today and every day, to help your kids fly?

REAL WORLD ASSIGNMENT:
Authenticity

We all "fake it" at times and that's not automatically bad. For example, pretending to be delighted when neighbors show up uninvited, teaches your children to be a gracious host even when it's not necessarily convenient. Faking a good mood can sometime help us get into a better mood! But pretending that what's going on around us is OK when it isn't, rarely leads to good choices. Neither does keeping our goodness locked inside because we're worried that our kindness will be mocked.

Listening In—The lessons we teach kids about expressing their feelings in healthy ways helps them discover who they ought to be. In this podcast (AnnieFox.com/podcast/FC020.mp3) from my series, Family Confidential (FamilyConfidential.com), I talk with David McQueen internationally known motivational speaker and founder of the Dave Mac Project, a unique teen empowerment movement based in the UK.

Fuel for Thought—Anne Frank famously wrote: "I keep my ideals, because in spite of everything I still believe that people are really good at heart." Think about the truly good-hearted people in your life. Might they agree with Anne

Frank? Do you? What's the connection (if any) between being a good person and seeing the good in others?

Conversations That Count—Talk with your child about a time when you were his age and wanted to fit in with the popular kids. Maybe you felt pressure to do something that didn't feel quite right. Ask your child, "What do you do in situations like that?" Then just listen and respond from the heart. Share what happened as a result of your long-ago choice to go along with the crowd. What did you learn about friendship? About yourself?

Teach—Effective immediately, make this offer to your child: "Any time you feel pressure to fake it and hide the goodness that I know is in your heart, come to me and we'll talk about what's going on. I may be able to help."

———————

WHAT WOULD YOU TEACH HERE?

I'm a guy and my best friend (a girl) was talking about pot. I promised I'd never smoke because I want to be in the Air Force but she said that she probably would because everyone does it. She's had crushes on guys who smoke, and I'm terrified of her getting into drugs. Lately we haven't been as close. It's almost like her personality has changed. She knows how anti-drug I am, and I'm afraid she won't tell me if she does it. What can I say to try and get her to stop smoking if I find out that she is? —13-year-old

Read my reply (AA 1.2)

SOMEONE IS ALWAYS NOT HAPPY

When we bought our house, part of the property was fenced in and part wasn't. We didn't mind, though, because the unfenced portion was adjacent to public open space, meaning that everyone has the right to enjoy the land and no one can build on it. Or so we thought. For twenty years, we boasted to out-of-town visitors how that land up there would forever remain untouched by contractors. Our bragging temporarily increased our Happiness Quotient (*aka* HapQ), as bragging often does. Though it probably decreased our guests' HapQ, which, now that I think about it, decreases my own. Sigh.

When a section of the ridge was sold (because it wasn't actually public land) we were not happy. When a massive house was built up there, directly above us, we were seriously bummed. But hey, no one can be happy all the time, right? So we breathed, let it go, and made our peace with the house on the hill.

Then, one day, my dog and I were hanging out by our bay tree. We were outside our fenced-in yard, but still on our own property. Suddenly our new neighbor swooped down like a Ringwraith with acid reflux. Admittedly, I've led a sheltered life, but I've watched enough reality TV to know that "Get off my $#@%$ property or I'll shoot your $#@%$ dog" qualifies as aggression. Adrenalin pumping, mind a blur, I hightailed it into my house, shaken and very emotional. Whoever said, "Words can never hurt me" was either a liar or a robot. Words can pierce your heart and set up camp in your mind where they continue to sting like time-released poison darts.

For the next two years, every time I stepped into my fenced-in garden, not daring to venture onto our own property outside the fence, the ghost of Ringwraith haunted me. I rarely saw my neighbor in the flesh, but his presence was palpable. His words tormented me, as did my own persistent fear and resentment.

Just at the point when I got fed up with myself for being stuck in this traumatized state, our apple tree died. Being a writer, naturally I had to delete it and hacked back the offending limbs. Unfortunately I lacked the muscle to finish the job, so the stump remained. Soon afterwards, the apricot tree also bit the dust. That's when I called the Tree Guy. He rid my garden of deadwood and planted a new apple tree. Delighted, I began dreaming aloud about extending the fence and enclosing all of our land in order to make a bigger garden with more veggie beds and fruit trees. Tree Guy, ever helpful, said, "No problem! My cousin is Fence Guy!"

After getting an official survey, Fence Guy showed up and Ringwraith reappeared, for real. Turns out he wasn't happy about our new fence and not shy about letting us know. My stress levels soared. But Fence Guy was philosophical. "Annie," he said with a shrug. "Someone is always not happy." True enough, but someone isn't always "not happy" with me and when they are, I become seriously unhinged.

As plans for the new fence proceeded, things with Ringwraith got increasingly dicey. He yelled. He bullied. And I drove to scary places in my mind, unable to find the off-ramp. I walked the hills. I breathed. I ate absurd amounts of very dark chocolate. I remained in child's pose for hours at a time. Nothing helped. Even after eight years of yoga and meditation I could not get happier. So I resorted to Annie-bashing. You heard me. Not only was I dealing with anxiety over an unhappy neighbor, plus my constant fear of his threatened reprisals, I was beating myself up for not being able to breathe my way back to Normal Life. My tower of unhappiness reached new heights and then added an impressive penthouse suite.

Then one day when . . . *presto*, life returned to Good.

I wish I could say I had a moment of enlightenment in which it became clear how I'd allowed fear to disable me so completely. But it didn't happen that way. We just built our fence and extended our garden as planned. When that went fence up, so did my Happiness Quotient. Oh, and we haven't seen our neighbor, lately. At this point I doubt it would bother me much if we did.

Soon after the fence was completed, I stood tall under a full moon, beside my bay tree. I felt strong and safe and completely at home. Was it really just a bunch of wooden posts and a few of rolls of wire that made the difference? Or had I somehow made myself safer by gradually realizing that I'd had it with being intimidated? I really can't say.

I also can't say exactly what all this has to do with teaching our kids to be good people. Except that sometimes we just have to tough it out in the face of bullies. And so do our kids. We can't always lift them up when they're down or stressed or scared. And they can't always cheer up their friends. At those times, maybe the best we can do is listen to what they have to say, empathize, and remind them that someone is always not happy. At this moment it's their turn. On the other hand, tomorrow might be their turn to smile. Just remembering that could help.

REAL WORLD ASSIGNMENT:
Intimidation vs. Self-Respect

We all feel vulnerable in certain everyday situations. If you know, for example, that spiders or elevators aren't your cup of tea, you can probably avoid them without much effort. But when there's an abusive person in our life who cannot be avoided, fear can keep us from enjoying peace of mind and making self-respecting choices.

Fuel for Thought—Chew on this quote by Anna Quindlen: "[W]hile we are supporting lessons in respecting others . . . remember that many of our youngest kids need to learn to respect themselves. You learn your worth from the way you are treated." How might your behavior signal to others "I'm OK with that" even when you aren't? What's the worse thing that has happened to you when you stood up for yourself? What's the best thing that happened?

Conversations That Count—Discuss with your child the meaning of the phrase "walking on eggshells" and the word "intimidation." We've all known people we've been reluctant to cross because of the intensity and unpredictability of their reactions. Talk about your experience with someone like that and what you learned. Encourage your child to talk about his experience with an intimidating individual (past or present). Ask, "If you could change something about your response, what would you change?" What advice can you give to help your child move in the direction of greater self-confidence and self-respect?

Teach—For a week, during the school commute or at dinner, or as an end-of-the-day ritual, take turns with your child filling in the blank in this sentence "Today I felt intimidated when _____." "Today I respected myself when _____."

––––––––––––––––

WHAT WOULD YOU TEACH HERE?

There's this guy I have a crush on. I'm not sure, but I think he likes me. My friend and I made up a great plan that on the last day of school before the bell, I will really quickly hug and kiss him on the lips like in a movie. I get so happy when I think of it. I am just scared that if I do he will not like me or pull away when I am kissing him. What do you think? Good idea or not?

—13-year-old

Read my reply (AA 1.3)

———————————

LOVE IS ALL WE NEED, SO WHY NOT ASK FOR IT?

Right before Thanksgiving a few years back, my dear friend Bettina, who was having some health issues, emailed me: "I know this is incredibly presumptuous and Miss Manners would be scandalized, but I'm wrangling for an invitation."

I was blown away. Not by her directness (God no!), but by the way she felt that she had no right to say, "I'm not feeling well and I don't want to be alone. Can I come over?" Immediately I called and thanked her for trusting me to understand her vulnerability. I also gave her top marks for the way she had honored herself by asking for what she needed. She was relieved to hear that she'd done the right thing by speaking up.

Most of us are much quicker to stand up for others than for ourselves. On some level we must believe we don't deserve to get our emotional needs met. But where does that foolishness come from? Here's my theory . . .

Babies are irresistibly cute so adults fall hard and take good care of them. Once they've gotten their sweet baby hooks into our hearts, they are experts at expressing their physical and emotional needs, nonverbally. As our children grow, our conversations with them center mostly on the physical aspects of life: *Sweetheart, are you hungry? Do you want something to drink? Is it nap time? Why don't you put on a sweater?* As a result, asking for tangible stuff is very easy for kids: *Dad, I need a ride. Mom, I need you to sign this. I need a new phone. I need money.*

Because most parents don't teach kids about expressing emotional needs, teens rarely say: *I need a hug. I need to share this exciting news! I need you to listen. I need you to tell me the truth. I need help.*

I asked a bunch of sixth–eighth graders to rate themselves on these two statements: "It's easy for me to ask for help" and "I pretend things are OK when they aren't." The results? Twenty-five percent of the kids said it was "never or almost never" easy to ask for help. Another 25 percent reported that "sometimes" they had trouble asking for help. And here's another sad finding: A whopping 83 percent admitted that "sometimes, always, or almost always" they pretend things are OK when they aren't.

An unwillingness to ask for help, coupled with a habit of pretending things are fine when they're not, is unhealthy. When we deny our human need to connect heart-to-heart, we end up short-changing ourselves and the people we're closest to.

A parent's role is to raise an emotionally healthy young adult. That includes helping a child recognize what s/he's feeling and learning to ask for support when needed. Of course self-reliance is essential and being able to calm yourself at times of stress is a life skill, but there's no denying that we all feel vulnerable at times. It's also true that we're all interdependent. When we let people know how we feel and allow them to love us and help us, we honor our humanity. We do the same when we love and help others.

On that Thanksgiving, my family and I were heading out of town, so our home was going to be cold and dark. I couldn't offer Bettina a warm place at our table. But with my encouragement, she was confident enough to express her needs to another friend who gladly opened his heart and home. What would surely have been a sad and lonely day for her, turned into a wonderful occasion. Less than two years later, Bettina died. Thinking about her, then and now, I'm comforted knowing that she wasn't alone on one of her last Thanksgiving holidays. She was brave enough to reach out and ask for what she needed. Bettina taught me a powerful lesson, especially important when we're vulnerable: When it comes to friends and family, hold nothing back. Allow yourself to love and be loved fully, without limits.

REAL WORLD ASSIGNMENT:
Taking Care of Emotional Needs

When we feel most vulnerable, we often resist asking for support. Instead, we simply fortify our "Everything's fine" act and endure in silence. Maybe we equate vulnerability with weakness or incompetence. Poor modeling for our children (*aka* "good people" in training)! Better to encourage them to advocate for their own needs and the needs of others.

Think—In which situations are you least likely to ask for needed help, comfort, and support? What have you taught your children, consciously or unconsciously, about asking for help?

Conversations That Count—Ask your child to rate himself on a scale of 1 to 5 (1=always, 2=almost always, 3=sometimes, 4=almost never, 5=never) for this statement: "It's easy for me to ask for help." Rate yourself. Share replies and talk about the personal challenges of asking for help. Discuss what prevents us from telling the truth when we aren't feeling sure about how to handle a challenge.

Teach—The next time your child is obviously upset, ask simply and directly, "How can I help you?"

NOTE: An open-ended question like "How can I help you?" (vs. "Can I help you?") or an observation like "You seem upset" empowers kids to think about what's going on and what they need. This also teaches them to tune in more closely to their emotions and to the needs of others.

WHAT WOULD YOU TEACH HERE?

Every time my boyfriend and I are with other people or we are out in public, he gets mad at me and says something like, "Fine! Then I'll just keep to myself." It really annoys me, but I don't know how to say something to him. —17-year-old

Read my reply (AA 1.4)

2: HOW SHOULD I KNOW WHAT TO DO?

DOING THE RIGHT THING IS GOOD KARMA

"Non-violence leads to the highest ethics, which is the goal of all evolution. Until we stop harming all other living beings, we are still savages."

—Thomas A. Edison

We are quick and infinitely creative when it comes to standing, sitting, or texting in judgment of others. A mere micro-synapse exists between unkind thoughts (*He's crazy! She's a bitch! Stupid move! Ugly!*) and actually saying something offensive. When we do speak with contempt, we know it's petty and well, yes, cruel, but we justify our behavior by convincing ourselves that the person we're targeting deserves it because . . . (see above judgmental thoughts).

These cutting remarks wound (which is probably why they're called "cutting"). They also pollute and damage family life and school culture. Teaching kids to be good people includes helping them see that *US* vs. *THEM* is a myth. We are all *US*. And there are no justifications for being mean. None. Of course, from time to time, our kids might still get into conflicts with others, but when they consider crossing the line, our voice needs to be inside their head. That just might give them enough lead-time to delete that barb before they press SEND.

DON'T ADD
TO THE GARBAGE

Up our street lies Faudé Park. Undeveloped except for some narrow trails carved into the hill, this 13.5 acre community treasure offers a mini-retreat to everyone wandering through. When David and I first ventured up to Faudé's highest point, we were delighted by the knockout view of Mt. Tamalpais. We were also depressed by the thick carpet of broken beer bottles tossed by partygoers who obviously enjoyed the "natural" environment. (A trashcan sits 20 feet from the peak. But hey, the ground's handier, right?)

David and I aren't neat freaks. Far from it. But we hated seeing all that glass in such a beautiful setting, so we started cleaning it up. The first day we spent 30 minutes picking up the biggest chunks of glass. When we returned a week later, new chunks replaced some of what we removed. But we weren't deterred. Over the next several months, we kept picking up glass.

At some point things began to change. Weekend revelers stopped tossing bottles on the ground. Maybe because they could now see the ground! Or maybe the beauty of the park became apparent and now they decided it wasn't cool to mess it up. Can't say for sure, but whatever the reason, David and I were happy with the change and didn't mind taking a little credit for getting things rolling in the right direction.

Turns out the trends we observed at the park reflect a bona fide sociological phenomenon called the broken windows theory. Apparently, the more rundown a neighborhood becomes, the more likely people will break windows in abandoned buildings, graffiti walls, and litter. The crime rate increases too. Conversely, when a neighborhood gets cleaned up, everything improves.

The turnaround at Faudé Park happened years ago, but I'm pleased to report that as of my walk this morning, the overlook is still totally free of garbage. Of course, not all garbage is equal, and the kind infecting most schools, *aka* social garbage, is of the invisible yet more toxic variety.

I frequently ask students: "If you walk into a room already littered with trash, is it OK to toss your candy wrapper on the floor?" Some kids will say, "Sure, it's OK." Why? Because "everyone else is doing it and you won't get in trouble."

Then I ask, "If the floor is clean, is it still OK to toss your trash?" Now most kids will say no. But a few kids are likely to let me know it's never OK to add to the garbage. Which is when I switch the discussion from candy wrappers to rude comments, rumors, and the rest of the social garbage many kids slog through every day.

A school's mission statement typically mentions something about respect and social responsibility. But how are schools teaching these values to their students? How are we, as parents, teaching them to our kids? We want them to grow into thoughtful, compassionate young adults who take time to think about their choices before they act, hopefully reflecting: "If I really want less garbage at school and at home, what can I do? Am I willing to watch my mouth and keep more hurtful comments to myself? Am I willing to stand up for someone being teased? Am I willing to speak out against demeaning 'jokes'? Willing to sincerely apologize when I mess up and hurt someone? Willing to reach out to someone who needs a friend?"

As I see it, the goal of effective parenting (aside from keeping your kid alive and well), is to help him develop a code of ethics. If you want your child to become a good person whose actions demonstrate a high level of personal integrity, if you want her to help promote more friendship, peace, and justice in the world, you need a plan.

Character development is an ongoing process for each of us. We have to consistently work through all these issues with our kids and our students, our colleagues and our partners. Talk about ethical behavior where you see it and where you don't. Model it in your own life. Help children evaluate their choices and learn from their mistakes. Help them deal with intense emotions in appropriate and responsible ways so they don't intentionally hurt other people.

There are no easy answers here, but one thing is for sure, the world desperately needs less garbage.

REAL WORLD ASSIGNMENT:

Respect

The "climate" within a family is maintained through the choices we make, moment-by-moment. We actively contribute to a hostile climate by showing contempt. We passively contribute to social garbage by choosing to turn a blind eye to negativity. Creating a more accepting, respectful climate is also a choice.

Listening In—As parents, we are our children's #1 Influencer and we want to make sure we use our influence for good. In this podcast (AnnieFox.com/podcast/FC017.mp3), I talk with superstar educator Salome Thomas-El (*aka* Principal El), author of *The Immortality of Influence: We Can Build the Best Minds of the Next Generation* (Dafina Kensington, 2006).

Fuel for Thought—If a hidden video camera recorded your family's typical interactions, what would it capture? Take the point of view of an observer. Focus on the way adults and kids in your family speak to each other. That includes the choice of words, tone of voice, volume, and attitude, as well as all expressions of nonverbal communication. What might your kids be learning at home about the way to treat people?

Conversations That Count—Call a family meeting (QT 2.1) for the purpose of discussing the concept of social garbage and how it applies to the climate within your family. Print and hand out copies of this Family Climate Questionnaire (QT 2.2). As much as possible, everyone (including the adults) should fill out the questionnaire independently. There are no right or wrong answers, so encourage honesty!

Teach—Share your questionnaire answers with each other. Make it 100 percent safe to discuss how the evaluations reflect each person's experience. Model respectful listening. After everyone has had their say, brainstorm some new family rules to help shift the family climate in the direction of more respect and less garbage. Post the new rules. Praise compliance and show appreciation for progress. When someone slips up (it will happen), respectfully hold people accountable. While a family is not a true democracy, we must be willing for our children to remind us when we accidentally add to the garbage. (Oops!) We're here to learn as well as to teach.

WHAT WOULD YOU TEACH HERE?

I like a guy who is always so mean to me. I used to pretend the things he said didn't hurt because if I made a problem out of it I could risk losing him. Then he deleted me as Facebook friend and I was really hurt by it, I still am. I tried having a conversation with him, but he never replied. So I wrote again saying that I at least don't want to leave things on bad terms and that I didn't hate him or anything. He never replied to that one either. I'm constantly checking my inbox, but nothing's ever there. I need to get over him because, in all honesty, he is such a horrible person to me. But it's hard to get over someone you see five days a week. —14-year-old

Read my reply (AA 2.1)

WHY LET THE TRUTH GET IN THE WAY?

We seem to live in a time and place where only a certain kind of fool admires honesty. Not ashamed to admit I am that kind of fool. Maybe you're reading this book about teaching kids to be good people because you're foolish in the same way. Like me, you may be naively shocked when you hear how someone in the corporate world, or in sports, government, journalism, etc., got to the top by cheating.

Dishonesty plays out most publicly during political campaigns where all it takes is money to distort or fabricate the truth. In 2008, Professor Michael X. Delli Carpini, Dean of the Annenberg School for Communication, pointed out that in the last two election cycles, "the very notion that the facts matter seems to be under assault." He went on to say, "Candidates and their consultants seem to have learned that as long as you don't back down from your charges or claims, they will stick in the minds of voters regardless of their accuracy, or at a minimum, what the truth is will remain murky, a matter of opinion rather than fact." That hasn't changed in 2012. Of course all this duplicity filters down from people in the spotlight to the rest of us—from adults to kids.

From Tom Sawyer's whitewashing scam to test taking, kids have always tried to find the easy way out. But in the past, when they got caught, responsible adults let them know, in no uncertain terms, that cheating is not acceptable. There were also consequences to drive home the ethics lesson. But today we seem to operate by a different set of standards. Our technology makes cheating ridiculously simple and more and more students push the boundaries of what is right, fair, and honest. I'm not shocked to hear of students plagiarizing from the Internet and using cell phones to cheat off of during tests.

However, I am surprised to hear that 25 percent of teens in a national survey don't consider sneaking peeks at cell phone notes during exams as cheating. And yes, I was stunned by news of a group of high-achieving students who recently developed an SAT scam where less academically gifted "clients" paid the whiz kids thousands of dollars to take the college entrance exam in their place. And the topper may be the fact that I am still (yes, still) blown away to hear of parents threatening lawsuits when schools attempt to discipline young cheaters. These same parents are privately berating their kids—not for cheating, but for getting caught!

Several years back I consulted for an educational publisher. Part of my job included exhibiting products at conferences and answering questions from the teachers in attendance. At the end of one long weekend, I discovered that several of our expensive books had mysteriously walked out of my booth. I couldn't believe they were gone. I remember the words spinning in my head, "Teachers stole the books?! How can that be?! Teachers don't steal!"

Surprise! Turns out that some teachers do. As do so many adults who, in one way or another, seem to succeed very well thank you, by using a different moral compass than the rest of us foolish naïfs.

What are we teaching our children about the value of being honest and trustworthy? If we choose to hold our kids to a higher standard of ethics, are we preparing them for real world success or inevitable, second tier status? Will an "unenhanced" performance be remembered as "an honest but failed attempt" while the guy who did whatever it took to win ends up with all the goodies? How do we teach the value of the long honest journey when so much of our culture values shortcuts?

REAL WORLD ASSIGNMENT:
Integrity

When kids get the message that their best isn't good enough unless they take home the gold, how can we be surprised when they break the rules to get what they want (including our approval)?

Fuel for Thought—Where did you learn your values regarding personal integrity? When a cashier or waitperson makes a mistake in your favor, how do you typically respond? Would you respond differently if your child were with you? Think about a recent time when your integrity was tested? What happened? What did you learn?

Conversations That Count—Discuss the concept of "personal integrity" (*adherence to moral and ethical principles; soundness of moral character; honesty*). To make the concept real, share examples with each other of when you stuck with your principles as well as instances when you let your principles

39

slip. Discuss what you learned when you did and did not live up to your own standards. Together, explore the connection between integrity and trust and what can happen when we find out someone we trusted hasn't been trustworthy.

Teach—Check in regularly with your child about tests of his/ her personal integrity at school and online. Creating a safe place to talk about ethical challenges helps kids gain confidence in processing options and doing the right thing.

———————————

WHAT WOULD YOU TEACH HERE?

My 16-year-old daughter is an honor roll student and top athlete, but since she's been hanging with kids I disapprove of, she's getting into trouble. She gave schoolwork to a boy to copy then lied to the school that she'd left her notebook and the boy picked it up and copied. She lied to us about sleeping at a girl friend's home then went to a boy's home whose parents were away. The police came and found alcohol and a bong. She has so much potential, but I'm afraid she'll keep making bad choices. —My child's teacher

Read my reply (AA 2.2)

41

DOING THE RIGHT THING IS ITS OWN REWARD, RIGHT?

Jonah Lehrer's bestseller, *How We Decide,* caught my eye in a Washington, D.C., bookstore. I'm fascinated by the way teens think when they're amongst their peers and doing their damnedest not to attract disapproval. I know that the teen brain often works against rational thinking. Developing brain matter is notoriously poor at impulse control, planning ahead, and being able to predict the outcome of one's choices. So when it comes to peer harassment, for example, when your typical middle schooler is angry, she isn't likely to stop and think, "I want to get back at that kid, but this mean stuff I'm about to post is probably going to hurt him a lot more than he hurt me. That's not fair. I'd better not do it." Bottom line . . . being thoughtful and rational during emotional times can be a monumental challenge for kids of all ages.

A book about decision-making in tough moments fits right in with my ongoing exploration of why good kids, who know the difference between right and wrong, often harass and bully each other. Instantly I decide to buy *How We Decide.*

A few days later, I'm reading a chapter about credit card spending and I have a major insight about bullying. (Stick with me for minute.)

Apparently when we buy something with cash we simultaneously feel a loss in the part of the brain associated with pain. "OW! There goes some of my money!" Because it hurts, people who pay with cash are less likely to make large impulse buys that can put them in a deep hole.

Conversely, brain-imaging experiments indicate that paying by credit card reduces feelings in the pain region of the brain and provides instant reward. ("I get what I want NOW!") In other words, when we buy with plastic we don't feel as bad so we tend to spend more without thinking about how we'll pay it back. In the peak year of 2009, Americans spent $22.9 billion in credit card penalty fees (including interest on unpaid balances). Ouch!

Now, back to bullying. If a boy cruelly mocks another child, face to face, he'll actually see the hurt he's caused and (hopefully) feel some "pain" in the brain. Because we're not big on punishing ourselves, this boy is less likely to harass that kid again. But when an aggressive child regularly texts vile, threatening messages, his bullying, like credit card spending and drone warfare, becomes an abstract, "painless" habit. Thus the bully will likely keep it up, especially when there's a reward. And there usually is! When it comes to gossiping with a friend vs. taking the high road and choosing not to add to the garbage . . . the choice is clear to the typical seventh grader. When he encourages a friend's meanness (by dishing with a peer) he gains popularity points. And that, my friends, is currency he can take to the bank!

In a typical middle school, where peer harassment is rampant, what's the reward for not engaging in malevolent behavior? What's the reward for being a truly nice kid? Until schools come up with the answer to that one, most kids aren't likely to choose doing the right thing over being popular.

Updated ethics lesson: In July 2012, best-selling author Noah Lehrer admitted that his most recent book *Imagine: How*

Creativity Works (2012, Houghton Mifflin Harcourt) contained quotes he attributed to Bob Dylan that "either did not exist, were unintentional misquotations, or represented improper combinations of previously existing quotes." I wonder how Lehrer decided that was OK? In short order his publisher recalled all the unsold copies of the book and the writer resigned from his position at *The New Yorker* magazine.

REAL WORLD ASSIGNMENT:
Decision-Making

Like every skill, decision-making takes practice. Ethical decision-making takes even more practice. Sometimes the decisions we make in a split second are exactly the ones needed to make the world (and our personal corner of it) a safer, saner, more compassionate place. But sometimes, even when we agonize for hours (or days) none of our options feel right, especially when we're worried about how our peers will react.

Fuel for Thought—When it comes to interacting with peers, some of us tend jump right in with our response to what's being said. Others tend to be more reflective, taking time to assess a situation before weighing in. Because life unfolds on a case-by-case basis, neither approach will be the best in all situations. How might your typical way of dealing with peers influence the way your child is learning to make social decisions?

Conversations That Count—Knowing the right thing to do in social situations and doing it are two very different animals. Ask your child: "Since most kids know it's not OK to be mean, what's your best theory about why there's there so much bullying in schools?" As your child thinks about this and shares his/her ideas, make sure you listen more than you talk. See where your child's thinking and experience lead the conversation.

Teach—If your child could benefit from spending more time thinking things through before he acts (at home, at school, online), then it's up to you to consciously model more reflective behavior. If your child tends to overthink things and gets bogged down and unable to make an ethical decision, try to model more "thoughtful spontaneity" (i.e., cutting to the chase without sacrificing personal integrity). Be on the lookout for teachable moments where you and your child can deconstruct and learn from a past decision or a current dilemma.

———————

WHAT WOULD YOU TEACH HERE?

I found out my son pressures girls for "second base" and if they don't comply, he dumps them. His last girlfriend told people he dumped her because she would not put out, but some girls go along with his demands! I am a single mom and I'm very upset to have raised a boy who'd do this to girls. How should I talk to him about this?

—My child's teacher

Read my reply (AA 2.3)

BULLY, THE MOVIE: HOW ABOUT SOME SOLUTIONS?

In an opening scene of the 2012 documentary *Bully*, a kid with an ice pack on his head and a shaken expression is asked by his school principal, "Oh, what happened to you?" To which the kid replies, "Johnny shoved my head against a nail."

School principals see and hear a lot during a typical day, and much of it is innocuous. As administrators they need to differentiate between "drama" and the real stuff or they'd have trouble staying sane. An upset child with an ice pack requires attention, so the principal in film briefly examines the kid's head and blithely reports, "Well, I don't see a hole." Spoiler alert: There's not going to be a whole lot of empathy coming from this administrator. I was half-expecting she'd say, "And what did *you* do to make Johnny so mad?" Instead she shooed the kid off to wherever. Another bullying incident swept aside.

The whole audience in that screening seemed frustrated by much of what we saw in *Bully*. The scenes with kids being targeted were compelling. I winced, I hid my eyes, I cried. But mostly, my fellow moviegoers and I sat incredulous at the consistent insensitivity of folks who are responsible for the safety and well-being of children.

Which brings up the scenes on the school bus. I've seen horrible acts of violence filmed by unmanned security cameras on buses, but the bus footage in *Bully* was made by the filmmakers! They kept filming while a child (Alex) was being pushed, hit, shoved, choked, and stabbed with a pencil over a period of days. I watch nature documentaries and I understand that filmmakers do not interfere with the "natural order" of things out on the savanna. If the lion catches the gazelle, the camera rolls on. But nothing is more repugnant than a film crew standing by while a *child* is being hurt. At one point it must have become too much for them because they put up an intertitle saying, "Because the violence was escalating and we were concerned for Alex's safety, we showed the footage to his parents and the school administration."

What the hell took them so long?! When Alex needed help they were apparently more concerned about their movie.

The film had its moments. Who could remain unmoved by a memorial service for a child? Or by a parent choking on her broken heart as she describes the angelic boy who was her son until she found him hanging from a rope in the tree? But these tragedies, reported in communities across the country, do not inspire real change in schools that need changing. That's why I've had it with feel good rallies, candlelight vigils, motivational message t-shirts, plastic bracelets, and balloon releases.

We are trying to teach our kids to be good people and we hoped *Bully* would provide some valuable solutions. But aside from the courageous leadership and determination of the parents of two of the targeted kids, the film didn't offer much inspiration. Without inspiration sometimes it's hard not to join the chorus of those who say, "Kids will be kids. There's nothing we can do about their behavior, so let them work it out themselves."

REAL WORLD ASSIGNMENT:
Going Along with the Crowd

We are wired to take our cues from the people around us. So it can be a challenge, even for adults, to buck the social system and take an unpopular stand. Imagine how much harder it can be for a child amongst his peers. But teaching your kids to be good people includes helping them to think independently.

Fuel for Thought—Recall a time you were dead set on something simply because "everyone" was doing it. Recall a peer-pressurized experience that pushed you into a decision you later regretted. If your parents found out, how did they handle it? What did you learn from your experience?

Conversations That Count—Introduce the term *sheeple* to your child. Sheeple are people who act like sheep. They're most comfortable following other people's rules of "acceptable" behavior, not allowing doubts about ethics to get in the way. The Golden Rule for Sheeple: "Thinking for yourself and being your own person is way too risky! Play it safe. Follow the others." Answer the questions on this Sheeple Quiz (QT 2.3) as you think your child would answer or as you would have answered when you were his/her age. Ask your child to answer the questions (independently). Talk about your answers and what, if anything, you'd each like to change in your behavior with peers. Help each other become more accountable in the areas of leadership and independent (ethical) thinking.

Teach—Be a leader so your child can learn what leadership looks like. (They are already getting enough lessons about how to be a sheeple.) Get into a habit of sharing "leadership" moments with each other. Give yourselves kudos whenever you did the right thing despite what the rest of the herd was up to.

WHAT WOULD YOU TEACH HERE?

Most parents don't want their kids to go with the crowd, but my daughter does the opposite. She dresses like a boy, only wearing boys' shorts and shirts. She isn't boy crazy, that's a good thing. It is beyond being a tomboy. She won't ever put her hair up like the rest of the girls, even though the coach tells her to. Does she want to stand out, or is she fighting the establishment? I want her to be herself, but she's way overboard and has no friends because she is so different. Should I just let her learn the hard way? —My child's teacher

Read my reply (AA 2.4)

3: HOW CAN I HELP?

FIGURING OUT WHAT'S NEEDED AND PROVIDING SOME OF IT

"The best advisers, helpers, and friends, always are not those who tell us how to act in special cases, but who give us, out of themselves, the ardent spirit and desire to act right, and leave us then, even through many blunders, to find out what our own form of right action is."

—Phillip Brooks

We enjoy being helpful because we are wired to reach out and try to make things better for others, especially the people we love. Our instinct to help comes from being social creatures. On a deep level we know that our survival depends on our cooperating with one another. Because we are natural helpers, it's not difficult to nurture a child's generosity. Yet 21st century culture can turn warm hearts cold, when, for example, we get a SPAM request from some unknown person whose "suffering" can be eased only if we "immediately wire $1500 to this account." On the flip side, technology inspires our good intentions by connecting us with opportunities to help those in real need. Teaching kids to be good people includes helping them develop a willing spirit paired with good judgment to assess what is truly needed.

SOME KIND OF HELP

"Auugh! I don't get this stupid homework!!!" your seventh grader wails. Devoted parent, you rush in and . . . do what? What kind of help is the right kind? Depends on your endgame, right?

Your basic job description: "Prepare your child to become an independent, fully functioning young adult." (If you've never read that anywhere, look at the bottom of your kid's birth certificate. It's there in the fine print.)

So . . . when your daughter groans or your son bellows, your most helpful move should be in the direction of supporting and encouraging them to work things out on their own. If your brand of "help" means you're doing the heavy lifting, crisis after crisis, year after year, you're not being all that helpful.

But we are parents and we like helping our kids. Of course, we do. In fact, on a cellular level, we're programmed to help and coach them, which is how they learn. And if we want them to grow into cooperative, good-hearted people, we start by helping them. That shows them what helping looks like and what it feels like to be on the receiving end of a helpful act.

Well-intentioned as our help may be, the "Let me tie your shoes" variety isn't supposed to last forever. Each time we help a child, we ought to provide instructions for identifying the problem, thinking through options, and making smart choices. That way, the next time, that child is more likely to resolve the challenge on his own, wisely and with confidence.

But when the only tool in a child's problem-solving kit is "get Mom/Dad to do it," it's harder to develop the skills and self-esteem that comes from being independent and responsible. Seems obvious, right? But less obvious is the fact that when we rush in with solutions, we might also teach kids they aren't capable of helping themselves or anyone else. Let's think about that one.

If I'm a kid who routinely turns to Mom/Dad, who is all too happy to "save the day" (again), I may start believing that I'm helpless, hopeless, and useless. I might resist tackling my own problems. ("I never do it right.") I may also hold myself back from stepping up and helping others. ("Why bother? I'll just make things worse!")

To teach kids the value of helping, we need to catch them in the act of following their kinder instincts. Let them know that what they just did for you, their sister, their friend, was very cool and you're proud of them. When they're stumped or frustrated, we need to resist the urge to jump in. Instead, we encourage them onward while we step back, little by little. Celebrate their "I did it!" moments and they will eagerly look for other things they can do on their own.

Will kids who are more independent need us less? Well, yeah! From the very beginning, that's always been the point of this parenting gig. We taught them how to walk and . . . they started walking away from us. It's true, they won't always need us, but they will always use what we taught them. And while we're teaching them self-reliance, we're also reinforcing our perception that they are the kind of people who care about others. Our perception of them colors their self-perception. We are teaching them that compassion translates into help and being helpful is what we're all here for.

REAL WORLD ASSIGNMENT:
Moving Toward Independence

Teaching children to be good people includes helping them sort things out on their own. Independent (ethical) thinking and action begins by teaching them to be their own problem-solvers. When we reinforce helplessness in our children, by doing for them what they ought to be doing for themselves, we make it harder for them to become independent young adults.

Listening In—Sometimes what we say we're teaching our kids is at odds with our parenting choices, especially when it comes to helping children develop self-reliance and learn to do the right thing. In this podcast (AnnieFox.com/podcast/FC001.mp3), I talk with Joe Bruzzese, M.A., author of *A Parents' Guide to the Middle School Years* (Celestial Arts, 2009).

Fuel for Thought—Some of our own parents weren't available or helpful enough while we were growing up. Others hovered, without providing enough breathing room for us to make our own choices. When teaching kids to be independent, a middle road approach can be effective—i.e., increasing independence year by year, with a decreasing parental safety net. What was your parents' approach to raising independent children? What have you taken from what you learned? Take this quiz: **Assumption or Fact?** (QT 3.2) to examine what assumptions you have about teaching kids to be self-reliant. Then check out this **Assumptions Toolkit** (QT 3.3) to help you deconstruct any assumptions that might be undermining your parenting efforts.

Conversations That Count—Talk to your child about his growing need for independence. Ask your child, "In what specific areas do you feel ready for more independence?" Working toward a new level of independence in mini-steps, respects a child's increasing maturity. It also encourages him to align his behavior with your clear expectations. When you grant a request for more independence make sure it's accompanied with an agreement about responsibility and accountability. Hold your child accountable for keeping his agreements. Hold yourself accountable for keeping yours. **Teach**—Rather than rewarding your child by instantly complying with every request for help, switch things up. Say, "Instead of hearing so much about problems, I want to hear more about solutions you've come up with on your own." Help her get into the habit of giving you an end-of-the-day "report" on the challenges she's worked through. Share some of your daily successes with her. To help kids develop independent problem-solving skills, we need to show them how we tackle our challenges and offer kudos for their efforts in dealing with their own.

WHAT WOULD YOU TEACH HERE?

My parents give me allowance, but not enough. Since I go out with girls I need money. I also need gas money for my motorbike. My dad understands, but my mom doesn't let him give me more money. I earn extra cutting the grass for neighbors. But these little jobs aren't enough for getting all the money I want. I came to the extreme point of stealing from the supermarket but I was caught. Now my parents don't give me any more money. My mom won't talk to me. I am very sad. —16-year-old

Read my reply (AA 3.1)

NEED SOME HELP, MOM?

Not too long ago I read a letter to Dear Abby from a distraught martyr . . . oops! I mean a mother who signed off as "Alone in the Kitchen." She plaintively described how her adult daughters arrive for the holidays each year expecting the guest treatment. For some mysterious reason, these two able-bodied young women never think to offer dear old Mumsie any help with the annual banquet she produces for 20+ guests. Their work avoidance goes on for a day or two until Mom, frazzled and frantic, slumps to the linoleum and whimpers like a pathetic dog. At which point the princesses roll their eyes and deign to lift a sponge for a fleeting moment, before trotting off and abandoning Mom again.

As I read the column, my blood pressure spiked with frustration. But my target wasn't the daughters as much Mom. I mean, really, where did she think her lovelies learned to act like guests at home? How in the world had they reached adulthood totally lacking the common courtesy to pitch in?

Abby called out Mom for overindulging, but I gave her answer a C+ because she neglected to offer Mom any suggestions for fixing the problem. If it had been my column, here's what I would have said:

> Dear Alone in the Kitchen,
>
> Wondering where Drizella and Anastasia picked up their royal sense of entitlement? Look in the mirror because it's self-reflection time. If you really want to change the dynamic in your family this holiday season and

forevermore, start with an apology. I'm serious! You have failed to teach your children the first thing about being helpful. Instead, you've taught them that their job is to sit back and let you cater to their needs. You've also held them back from developing a cooperative spirit by rewarding them for being self-centered. Admit the ugly truth. Forgive yourself. Apologize. And move forward, quickly, because you've got a turkey to stuff!

In friendship,
Annie

There are always things that need to be done to make a home livable. (Of course, it's our living in it that makes it messy, but we can't get around that, can we?) Whether you're prepping for a special family event or needing to dive into seasonal household chores, make a master task list. Gather the troops, post the document, and announce to your family, "Here's what needs to get done. Which tasks are you taking responsibility for?" (Speak as assertively as possible. No shouting, asking, pleading, guilt-tripping, etc.) If you have no confidence in someone's promise to help (due to past flakiness) then get it in writing. After each self-selected assignment, smile, and in your best coach voice say, "Thanks. We're all counting on you."

My personal, unscientific research clearly indicates that when we want something done, the chance of compliance drops to less than 20 percent when our request comes in the form of a spineless question like "Can someone please help me?" ("No thanks.") "Can I ask you a favor?" ("Sure, but I'm not doing it.") "Do you have a minute?" ("Not now.") See what I mean? Instead, try this: "Hey guys, I need some help in here." See? It's a statement, not a question. Practice it on your own so there is no trace of pleading in your voice.

Breaking patterns isn't easy, but it's easier than breaking your back doing all the work with little or no cooperation from anyone. It's also better for your soon-to-be young adults to learn to notice the needs of others—essential in teaching them to be good people.

As for any male or female martyrs within the sound of my voice, that would be anyone who believes if s/he doesn't do it all single-handedly, s/he won't be a "good" parent, nor be loved and appreciated: You are already loved, appreciated, and admired. And when it comes to holiday celebrations, if you do much more than your fair share, you may end up with a sore back and feelings of resentment, and where's the holiday spirit in that?

So teach your children to help. Otherwise, how can they possibly learn to make a killer Thanksgiving dinner on their own some day? And how will they teach your future grandkids to be helpful people at home and out in the world?

———————————

REAL WORLD ASSIGNMENT:
Help Is a Two-Way Street

When we constantly give to our kids and require nothing of them as members of The Team, *aka* our family, they'll likely assume they should always be on the receiving end of life's goodies. Teaching kids to be good people includes helping them learn that we are all here to help each other. Which makes the question, "Do you feel like helping me do the dishes?" seem like a query from Mars. It implies no awareness of what being part of a family means. It also assumes that deciding to help someone we love is based on our mood rather than the fact that kindness is our natural go-to place.

Fuel for Thought—Recall your feelings, as a child, when you helped your family. Maybe it included emptying wastebaskets, raking leaves, setting the table. Or maybe a sibling, parent, or grandparent needed extra help and you were consistently there for them. In what ways do you expect your children to help? In what ways might you be shutting them out of the process, assuming they're "too young" (incapable) or that children should only "have fun."

Conversations That Count—Use the concept of "shared responsibility" to talk about helping life in your family run more smoothly. Work together to create a list of required daily, weekly, monthly tasks. Avoid the word "chore" and a martyr's tone as you and your child(ren) talk about who typically does what around the house. Skip blame and resentment and move forward as a team, thinking of ways to share the work more fairly with the goal of helping each other.

Teach—You are the leader of your family. A positive attitude gets more heartfelt cooperation than nagging or begging. (Remember, what Daniel Goleman says about creating "effective relationships.") We work together because we love each other. As a team we all benefit from (a good meal, a floor you can walk on without tripping, sorted socks, a happy dog, etc.). When divvying up the work, it's best when people choose what they'd like to do. If that gets everything divvied up, great! If not, rotate the tasks. To avoid memory lapses, document who has agreed to do what and hold yourself and others accountable. Work together. Listen to music. Laugh. Create cleaning races by setting a kitchen timer, and see how much you can get done in 10 minutes. The goal, as always, is progress, not perfection. Acknowledge the team effort and the positive results. Being persnickety about the way something "has to be done" dampens the group's helping spirit.

WHAT WOULD YOU TEACH HERE?

Our family is going through some tough times. My mom's stressed and works from 4:30 a.m.– 8:00 p.m. My dad needs lots of help because he has cancer. My older sisters live far away and have their own families. So I'm in charge. I cook, clean, and help my parents. I'm not exactly complaining, but add all that to homework! (Our teachers are really piling it on.) Please help me with a system to get stuff done fast!

—15-year-old

Read my reply (AA 3.2)

I'M STUCK!

When our kids are little, we actively teach them the importance of being nice to others. Most toddlers have been repeatedly commanded to "Share!" They usually comply—not because they're necessarily altruistic by nature, but because they know they'll catch it from Mom or Dad if they don't. As parents and as members of society, we have a vested interest in teaching children empathy, compassion, etc. But what happens to those lessons when they get older?

As peers play an increasingly vital and complex role in the lives of our adolescents, we should continue discussing these issues. If we have any doubts about the need, we only have to take a moment to recall how clueless we felt in middle school and how not knowing what to do in social situations caused us, and our peers, so much anguish. But for some reason, parents of middle and high school students don't often talk about what it takes to be a good friend and how to stand up for yourself when you're not being treated with respect.

When we don't teach our kids about respect and self-respect, they may find themselves in situations like this:

> Tina and Danielle have been best friends since second grade. Now as sixth graders, Danielle has been hanging out with the popular girls. Monday at lunch, Danielle was with her new friends. Tina tried talking to her, but Danielle made some joke about Tina's shoes and all the other girls laughed. That hurt, but Tina pretended it didn't bother her. On Tuesday Danielle ignored her old friend completely. At the end of the day Tina got up the courage to ask what was going on. Danielle just smiled sweetly and said, "What are you talking about?" Tina

thought that maybe she imagined the whole thing. On Wednesday morning, a couple of popular girls asked Tina why she was being so mean to Danielle. Tina's heart pounded as she denied it. The girls exchanged a knowing look and walked away. By lunch Tina's fate was sealed—not one girl in the sixth grade would talk to her.

What had Tina done to turn everyone against her? She'd broken a cardinal rule of tween/teen friendships: No matter how much your friend hurts or embarrasses you, do *not* stand up for yourself or you risk losing that friend. In other words, you don't have the right to help yourself in these situations. Huh? That's just nuts!

What happened to teaching kids to be assertive? What happened to helping them develop self-esteem and self-respect? What can parents do to help their daughters and sons stand up for themselves when friends aren't acting like friends?

I get tons of email from young people suffering at the hands of so-called friends. Just like their vast confusion about the Boyfriend/Girlfriend Zone, tweens and young teens don't understand how to maintain a healthy friendship. They pour out their hearts with tales of woe:

☞ "My friends aren't really my friends."
☞ "I don't know why they hate me."
☞ "My friend posted nasty things about me."
☞ "They said I was gay."

We've all suffered from friendship betrayals. Most of mine happened in the sixth- and seventh-grades, and they were devastating. So I can genuinely empathize with the kids. But my empathy, in and of itself, isn't much help. The only real help any caring adult can provide is letting kids know that they have choices. Silence is a choice. Pretending things are "fine" when they're not, is a choice. Staying in an abusive friendship or seeking revenge are also choices, albeit not very smart ones. Until kids realize when they are making unhealthy choices (or contemplating them) *and* they recognize that they have viable alternatives, they're going to feel stuck and helpless.

For several years I've been teaching friendship workshops to students in the third–eighth grades. While girls' friendship challenges can appear to be more emotionally draining, that may only be because, generally speaking, girls tend to talk more about their emotional lives. Boy friendships can just as easily turn mean and cause hurt feelings.

As a parent, you are a teacher. You don't need one of my workshops to help a child struggling in an unhappy friendship. In fact, you certainly don't need to wait until your daughter or son is having friendship problems to start teaching them that creating and maintaining healthy friendships requires a set of skills. By practicing the skills and realizing that both friends must be equally committed to the friendship, kids can learn to recognize the characteristics of a good friend, and later on down the road, they can take those lessons and apply them to the Boyfriend/Girlfriend Zone.

The most important thing for us to help our kids realize is that friendship is a two-way street. It's built on mutual trust, affection, respect, honesty, support, shared core values, and open communication. We want them to help themselves by speaking up when a friendship goes off track. The other part of the two-way Friendship Street is teaching kids to show respect to a friend by listening. Because let's be honest, sometimes it's our friend's behavior that needs a course correction, and sometimes the problem is us.

REAL WORLD ASSIGNMENT:
Resolving Inner Conflicts

Some relationship conflicts cause us such angst we haven't got the bandwidth to think things through. In those cases, we probably aren't aware of all of our options for resolving the conflict. Other times we know our options and we don't like any of them, especially if we're unwilling to upset the person who may be a key contributor to the conflict. Being unwilling or emotionally unable to do what's needed to change the dynamic, we can feel stuck in an uncomfortable limbo where the problem persists, as does our suffering. So frustrating and yet, so resolvable!

Fuel for Thought—Being assertive is a life skill and a key to learning how to help oneself. Think about times in your childhood, or more recently, when you really felt "stuck" in a relationship dynamic. What was going on? How did you resolve the dilemma? If you're still in the middle of it, what options do you have? What might be your next best move?

Conversations That Count—Talk to your child about feeling stuck. Discuss the benefit of waiting before making a move. (It often helps to calm down so we can do a better job of identifying our options and predicting the potential outcome of choosing A over B.) While it's never OK to be intentionally mean, sometimes making the right decision will result in someone's feelings getting hurt . . . even if we wish that weren't part of the deal. Speaking up for yourself is a good thing. Attacking someone else is not. Teach your child the difference between being assertive and aggressive.

Teach—Brainstorm remedies for getting "unstuck." Come up with some *hypotheticals* and practice acting them out. For example, a scenario about an adult dealing with a stubborn co-worker or a child in conflict with another child. Brainstorm creative ways to help each other identify those feelings of being stuck and how to deal with them. Then make a pact to support and encourage each other to get unstuck from these situations. Try this nine-step strategy (QT 3.1) for helping kids get unstuck.

———————————

WHAT WOULD YOU
TEACH HERE?

I know everyone thinks only girls get eating disorders, but I'm a guy and I think I have one and I need help. I eat half of a small energy bar before school, then I don't eat lunch. Then I eat the other half of the bar and some fruit. It's gotten to the point where I'm mad at myself if I even take a bite of food. I get a lot of hate from people calling me fat and pointing out every flaw I know I already have. My mom says, "I don't think you eat enough." I pretend I don't hear. People at school ask if I want some of their food and I say no thank you. I know they worry about me. I don't feel welcome anywhere I go. The Dean

71

of Students saw me and asked if I wanted to talk, but I said everything was fine. I know teachers worry about me because they watch me just sit there during lunch and not eat. I don't know what to do. I feel really stuck. —15-year-old

Read my reply (AA 3.3)

ON BECOMING A MORE TOLERANT, PATIENT HUMAN BEING (DAMMIT!)

Face it, the people we live with and love and cherish more than life itself can push our buttons like nobody's business. (That expression never made much sense to me but I've always enjoyed the sound of it.) Button-pushing fests can be especially aggressive between parents and teens. They give us one of those looks or some of that attitude and we completely lose it. Of course, on the flip side, we parents routinely do and say things that irritate the crap out of our children. Such is life, right?

But who are the adults here? I guess that would be us, but sometimes it's hard to tell. When I think about what some of my "moments" might have taught my daughter and son about self-control, conscious choice making, and treating others with respect, well, I want to call the Bad Parent Police. But in an out-of-control moment, instead of turning ourselves in, we need to forgive ourselves in the same way that we forgive our kids when they act . . . crazy. Then we've got to take stock of what we just did (or failed to do) and make a course correction for next time. (And you know there will be a next time!)

Each day can offer up never-before-seen challenges to our parenting chops. If you haven't yet reached human perfection, you might want to try this simple process. It can help you be more of the kind of parent you want to be more of the time—especially when someone in your family is being sooooo annoying.

73

When a family member does something that grates on your nerves, ask yourself: *What am I feeling right now? Irritated? Embarrassed? Frustrated? Angry?* Identifying what we're feeling is the first step to understanding our behavior and ourselves. When we step back and look at the emotional component of our behavior, we take our reactions off autopilot and bring them into the realm of conscious thought. Which, by the way, is the place in the brain from where we make our most effective and helpful parenting choices.

That first question (*What am I feeling?*) is relatively simple, so let's increase the challenge. Try to figure out: *Why does his/her behavior bother me so much?* If we're going to develop more control over our knee-jerk reactions, it helps to understand why our buttons get pushed. It might be that we just don't like or trust or even understand what the child is doing. At that moment, our Super Parent jumps in and takes over. Sometimes we need to jump in, but sometimes we are overreacting, and that's not helpful.

Next question: *When stuff like this happens, what's your usual way of responding? Does it add more or less stress? Does it help/aggravate the situation? (Be honest.)* Thinking clearly about our typical reactions to stressful situations can encourage us to explore other options. Especially if what we normally do tends to add fuel to the fire.

When people push our buttons, we just react. That's why they're called "buttons." But instead of simply reacting, how about pausing long enough to ask ourselves, *What does my child need right now?* If we can hop off the hamster wheel long enough to consider what's going on and how we might help, negative family dynamics may start to shift. For example, right now, does this person (my son/daughter/partner) need someone to listen to him and acknowledge his feelings? Sounds like what most of us need at times. So the problem may not be what he wants, but rather his inability to ask for it directly. If we can figure out what someone wants and can provide some or all of it, we might begin to experience a) less "annoyance" in the face of their behavior, b) more compassion and love, and c) more freedom from unhelpful automatic reactions. Win-win.

With empathy and a willingness to talk about feelings and needs, we teach our children that healthy adults can change and continue to grow in positive directions. Bottom line, just like our kids, we parents are also works in progress.

REAL WORLD ASSIGNMENT:
Patience

Sometimes our desire to help is snuffed out by our child's "bad" behavior. But acting out is often a sign that s/he needs our help more than ever. By developing the patience to look past the "unacceptable"* behavior, we can begin to recognize the universal human need behind it. When we do that, our compassion and willingness to help, returns in force.

*NOTE: When the unacceptable behavior is dangerous or in any way destructive to other people or to property, intervene to stop the behavior immediately. Do it as calmly and respectfully as possible. Then do your best to help your child examine the emotions that fueled the behavior.

Fuel for Thought—Think about a family member who has an irritating behavior. Image the behavior as a mask or a thin veneer, i.e., a superficial cover for a deeper more vulnerable need. What would it take for you to disregard the veneer long enough to figure out what the person really needs?

Conversations That Count—Talk honestly about the challenges we all have from time to time in expressing our needs and responding compassionately to the needs of others. Share what you've learned about being part of the family you grew up in. Remind your kids that families are forever, but family dynamics are not carved in stone. Just because people have always interacted in a certain way doesn't mean they can't change.

Teach—Identify one annoying behavior *of your own* and encourage your child to do the same. (We often know exactly what we do that irritates people and sometimes this opportunity to name "that thing I do" can be fun!) After you identify the behavior take it to the next level and think about why you do what you do. You might say, for example, "Sometimes when I do A, what I really want is B." (B might equal: attention, cooperation, peace, and quiet, the freedom to choose what I want to do next, etc.) Let your child know that you'd like to get better at asking for what you need and giving other people what they need. The next time you or your child does something "annoying," remind each other of this conversation and try to be more honest about what you really need.

WHAT WOULD YOU TEACH HERE?

When my 14-year-old son doesn't get his way, he starts yelling and cursing. He started getting physical with his father, my ex, and came to live with my second husband and me. Same problem. Last night my son got physically violent with me. Later he came downstairs, crying, and saying he was sorry. I think it would be good for him to talk with his youth minister, or has it gone too far and the authorities need to be brought into the situation? —My child's teacher

Read my reply (AA 3.4)

4: HOW ABOUT LETTING IT GO ALREADY?

RELEASING SHAME, REGRET, AND CONTEMPT

"You will make mistakes—it is inevitable. But once you do and you see the mistake, then you forgive yourself and say, 'Well, if I'd known better I'd have done better.' That's all. So you say to people who you

think you may have injured, 'I'm sorry.' And you say to yourself 'I'm sorry.' If we hold on to the mistakes, we can't see our own glory in the mirror because we have the mistake between our faces and the mirror; we can't see what we're capable of being."

—Maya Angelou

The thing about mistakes is that most of us don't deal with them in healthy ways—at least, not consistently. We often allow our mistakes and those of others to cloud our good judgment. And while it does no good to keep revisiting feelings of regret (if we offended someone and have already apologized) or resentment (if someone did it to us), frequently we continue holding on. Teaching our kids to be good people includes helping them forgive mistakes and focus on what is good in them and others . . . which is plenty!

———————

DAMN RIGHT
I'VE BEEN WRONGED!

Several years ago I collaborated, with a colleague, on a project from hell. By the end our yearlong working relationship, the two of us were barely speaking to each other, as in not at all. The final brick in the fortress was cemented in place when I hissed over the phone: "Let's just finish the damn thing." And we did, sorta. By which I mean, yes, we completed the project and delivered an award-winning result but no, we never successfully "finished" the real business between us. Not then and not in the intervening years.

Now, you may be thinking, "Oh, good! Annie's going to reveal her personal strategy for rising above the animus in a cantankerous relationship and letting one's Higher Angels guide us through. Now that's information I can use as I teach my kids to be good people." Sorry, but I'm not headed there so feel free to turn in your ticket stub at the box office for a full refund.

The truth is, I made things worse. During most of that wretched year and for at least two more afterwards, whenever the subject of this collaboration surfaced or I found a way to insert it into a conversation, I instantly morphed from a reasonable woman into an out-of-control victim who could not stop whining. Sigh. On the plus side, I'll give myself a bit of credit for refraining from airing dirty laundry whenever I functioned in any professional capacity. Minor kudos aside, I am not proud of the venom I spewed while boring my family and a few close friends with my rants. In fact, I'm mortified when I recall how I ran my mouth in front of my children! Not only was I stuck at a self-pity party, I kept gorging myself at the Outrage Buffet.

Why am I telling you all this? Because you're not the only one who (sometimes) gnaws on old rancid bones without letting up. We've all been upset enough to do it and so have our kids. Recalling my compulsive need to relive my precious feelings of hurt, betrayal, and resentment, I've gotta wonder, *Was I temporarily insane?* I must have been. What else explains all that rehashing? The first twenty helpings of that hash were bad enough. No doubt I could have processed the trauma in healthier ways and spared my captive audiences untold suffering. I sincerely apologize to you all, and to myself for being such a masochist.

Happily, that particular pity party has permanently left town . . . without me. But the next time I'm bonkers, blaming, and blathering endlessly about someone who has "done me wrong," I hope I have the wherewithal to stop, take numerous deep breaths, and cut to the chase with a few self-directed questions:

☞ *What happened?* (Just the facts, ma'am. Hold the editorial comments.)

☞ *How did my response contribute to the situation?* (Me?! Yeah, you.)

☞ *What (if anything) would I like to say or write to the person I'm complaining about?* (Always more effective and ethical than talking about him/her.)

☞ *The next time I'm in a similar circumstance, what might I do differently?*

Yep, that's what I'm going to do. Or at least I'm going to try. Promise. OK, folks, party's over . . . for now.

———————

REAL WORLD ASSIGNMENT:
The Pit of Self-Pity

When truly bad stuff happens it's common to feel unlucky, burdened, or cursed. But during one of those "It sucks to be me" moments, our challenges may not be all that earth-shattering. Of course, self-pity, by nature, fogs perspective. It also interferes with doing the right thing moving forward, the only direction Life actually travels. As Helen Keller said, "Self-pity is our worst enemy and if we yield to it, we can never do anything wise in this world." Teaching our kids to move past bad choices and old hurts is wise teaching, but we can't effectively teach it until we master it ourselves.

Fuel for Thought—If you ever stayed too long at your own guilt or self-pity party, the dregs of some negative feelings may still be influencing you. Imagine encountering someone you "wronged" or someone who "wronged" you. Are you OK making eye contact? Exchanging polite greetings? To the degree you'd rather not see him/her again, the emotional burden you're carrying might be holding you back from being as good a friend, partner, parent as you could be in your other relationships. (This stuff creates wide ripple effects.) What might you gain or lose by letting go of those negative feelings from the past?

Conversations That Count—Discuss with your child the concept of forgiveness (*releasing stockpiled emotions connected to what you've done or what others have done to you*). Talk about the idea of letting go of guilt, anger, etc., and moving on. Be clear with your child that linking Forgive and Forget is impractical. We can't just snap our fingers and choose to forget something (especially when it involves intense emotions) but we can decide how much hurt we will continue lugging around. That's a choice!

Teach—The next time your child is upset by a friend, or feeling guilty over some hurt s/he has caused, teach about forgiveness. What actually happened between the friends is Part A. How your child currently feels about it is Part B.

> **Part A**—Tell your child, "I see you're still upset with your friend. If you two haven't yet talked about this, you should. You two would get a chance to apologize. That might help clear up what happened. You could talk about why it wasn't OK. If you need help figuring out what to say, let me know."

> **Part B**—Ask your child to imagine wearing a backpack filled with the hurt (or guilt) s/he feels about what happened. "How many pounds are you carrying? Three pounds? Ten pounds? Two million tons?!" (Humor can sometimes help kids extract themselves from the pit of self-pity.) "You can carry that weight as long as you want, or you can choose to let some of it go. It's up to you. I'm always here to help you take care of yourself. Forgiveness is a good way to do it."

WHAT WOULD YOU TEACH HERE?

My best friend in the entire world is being very mean to me. He made a new friend last year and now he won't hang out with me. He never sits with me at lunch and seems embarrassed to talk to me. He's always with his new friend and I feel as if he is leaving me behind. I'm tired of coming home each day with hurt feelings. —11-year-old

Read my reply (AA 4.1)

_____

WHEN YOU'VE LOST SOMEONE'S TRUST

My emails from teens frequently involve questions about trust. Specifically "I'm a good kid who never does anything wrong, but my parents just don't trust me." Or "My dad promised he'd stop smoking, but he's said that before and I don't trust him any more." Or "I made one little mistake and now my parents won't trust me or give me another chance." In this essay, written for teens, I try to help them understand the fragile nature of trust and how what we promise and what we follow up with actually matters. I share it with you here, to help you help your sons and daughters understand that sometimes you don't get another chance to make things right.

When someone, especially someone close to you, entrusts you with personal, private information it probably makes you feel very special. And it should, because you care about that person and you want the trust between you to grow. And so, at their request, you promise not to betray their confidence. In other words, you swear you will keep your mouth shut and you totally mean it. And they trust you. But then, a while later, you find yourself talking to someone else and without meaning to hurt your friend, you tell the thing you promised you wouldn't! As soon as the words are out of your mouth you get that "Uh, oh. Maybe I shouldn't have done that" feeling. More often than not, things go downhill from there.

86

Has anything like this ever happened to you? It happened to this girl. Now she feels terrible and needs some help. So she wrote Terra (my online persona):

Hey Terra:

My boyfriend broke up with me because I lost his trust. I was telling people things he told me. For example he told me that he was really mad at his parents for grounding him and he was seriously thinking about running away. Then I told my friends. I thought my bf wouldn't mind me telling my friends because they are like best friends with him.

I regret that I told them anything. I want to gain his trust back but I don't know how to really "show" it. When I chat with him online he seems like he doesn't want to talk and that really annoys me. Today I was talking to him and he said that nobody could ever gain his trust back and that people only get one chance. I screwed up my chance. I really want his trust back again. I told him that but he said I should have thought before I acted. I'm not sure what to do!

Sorry Serena

Hi Serena,

We all make mistakes. (Welcome to the club!) But not everyone knows how to use a mistake to learn something positive and move forward with new wisdom. Hopefully you will.

When someone tells you they feel like doing something dangerous, like running away, a real friend tries to use her influence for good. You could have told your boyfriend, "If you're that angry, talk to your parents about it, but don't run away! That's nuts. You could hurt get seriously hurt. And your parents would be so worried. Don't do it!"

87

By telling other people what he said, you added to the social garbage in your school. Rumors start easily and people are easily upset. What you did wasn't helpful.

I admire your self-awareness and I respect that you're not making excuses for what you did. You're sorry and you sincerely apologized. That was the right thing to do. Something else you ought to do is try to remember what was going on in your head when you decided to tell your boyfriend's secret. Were you trying to impress your friends? Get someone in trouble? Stir up a little drama? If you're not sure why you did it, play back this "mental movie" in your head so you can figure out what made you think telling his secret was OK, even though you promised you wouldn't. Reviewing your own behavior in this way can help you avoid doing the same thing again. As for your ex not trusting you any more, well, maybe you can understand why he feels betrayed. His pulling away from you is a human response to protect him from being hurt or embarrassed again.

I understand that you'd like the relationship exactly the way it way before. But that's not going to happen right away. In fact, it may never happen. It takes time to build trust in a relationship and, as you've just experienced, all that can vanish in an instant when one person breaks a promise. The long road from betrayal back to trust is just that . . . a long road. Apologizing is the first step, but you can't simply apologize and talk your way back into someone's trust. Not if they aren't ready to trust you again. Your actions, over time, will either prove that you are trustworthy or not. And either he will choose to give you another chance or he won't.

My advice (since you asked) is that you forgive yourself for your mistake and continue to be the best, the most trustworthy friend you can be . . . to everyone. That's all you can do. The rest is out of your hands. No sense stressing about it. Just promise yourself that in the future you will try to be more aware of what you promise and what you deliver through your actions.

I hope this helps.

In friendship,

Terra

REAL WORLD ASSIGNMENT:
Trust and Betrayal

Mutual trust, the foundation of every healthy relationship, is built over time, through a series of thoughtful, considerate choices. Once trust is firmly rooted, we can relax and rely on the people close to us to mean what they say. Rash decisions, on the other hand, can make us seem untrustworthy. Even when we realize we've made a mistake, we may already have damaged a precious relationship, sometimes irreparably.

Fuel for Thought—Teaching kids to be good people includes helping them become trustworthy. Recall a time, in middle or high school, when you knowingly broke an agreement with your parents and they found out. How did they respond? If the response you got wasn't how you would have handled it (if you'd been the adult at the time) what would have been a more effective way to teach what you needed to learn?

Conversations That Count—Talk with your daughter/son about a friend's broken agreement. Choose a situation from a while ago, so the feelings of disappointment, betrayal, etc., aren't so raw and your child is more likely to think and speak rationally. Listen empathetically. Ask, "What did you learn from that?"

Teach—Families are the best place to learn about building trust. Yet many families have repeated disconnects when it comes to certain agreements. For example, Dad agrees to pick up son at 4:15 on Wednesdays, but rarely arrives before 4:35. Son agrees not to play computer games until homework is done, but he plays anyway. These *boomerang issues* keep coming right back and hitting us in the head. Agree that the next time the boomerang reappears, instead of seething or lashing out, you will talk about how it feels not to be able to trust one another to do what was promised. Ask, "What would it take to resolve this issue permanently and rebuild the trust in this area?" Don't shy away from this opportunity to teach and *learn*, Mom/Dad . . . especially if you haven't consistently kept your agreements.

WHAT WOULD YOU TEACH HERE?

My wife searched our kids' rooms (son 17, daughter 15). In our daughter's room we found over-the-counter sleep meds. My son is a wrestler and in his room we found what I think are Niacin capsules and laxatives. He has had prior trouble at home, not legal trouble, with marijuana . . . multiple times. I contacted his wrestling coach. How do we handle this? I feel that we need to confront both kids, but this would tell them we search their rooms and will only entice them to find better hiding places. —My child's teacher

Read my reply (AA 4.2)

MY (VERY BAD) BAD

My batting average for giving helpful advice is above .500. Like anything else, if you keep practicing you get better and I've been at my *Hey Terra!* online teen advisor gig since 1997, so I know I'm improving. But I don't always hit it out of the park. I really blew it recently and I'm going public because I want parents to know that even if you mess up royally on any particular day, you can give it another shot and try to redeem yourself. When you do, you're teaching your kids something very important about mistakes and forgiveness.

So here's my bad:

I got an email from "Confused" who described how she was masturbating a guy during class. Yes, you heard that right and I know what you're thinking. It made me crazy too! Which is exactly why I responded the way I did! But I'm getting ahead of myself. The girl wrote to me because she was afraid if she discontinued service the boy would "get mad." Her question to me: What do I do?

I wrote back:

Can I ask you a few questions so I can understand this situation better? Why did you think this was a good idea in the first place? (Just curious.) Now it seems like you've reconsidered and you don't think this is a good idea any more. What made you change your mind? One more question: Why is it so important that this guy continue assuming that you are the kind of girl who will do whatever he wants?

In friendship,
Terra

On the surface my response sounded reasonable, right? But just below the pixels on the screen I was *screaming* with justifiably righteous feminist indignation! And the girl picked it up immediately and wrote back how she regretted writing to me, didn't appreciate how I mocked her and busted me for being "unsupportive."

OW! That hit hard. I felt crappy. I mean, I've been doing this all these years because I want to help teens sort out their feelings when they're confused. I want to teach them to make healthy choices that reflect their Higher Self, not some pretend version they've mocked up just to get people to like them. If there's any ego involved in my online Q&A, it's the fact that I pride myself in offering nonjudgmental support. But I totally stomped on my own code of ethics when I judged that girl. She felt attacked and got defensive because I attacked her!

After I caught my breath, I wrote back:

Dear Confused,

Please forgive me for judging you. I was wrong and I apologize. I was trying to help you but I didn't express myself very well. I'd like to try again.

I'm glad you wrote to me and I respect you for it. I think it's important for you to get some help understanding why you got into this situation to begin with. Until you understand why you chose to do this then you are very likely to get into these uncomfortable situations again. I'm sure you don't want that.

As for getting out of it now, you can! Either you tell the guy, "I'm not doing that any more," and if he gets mad, so be it. OR you simply make it clear by the way you sit (with your hands away from him) that you're no longer going to do it. If he asks you what's going on, you can simply say, "Not doing that any more." End of conversation.

In any situation you find yourself, please remember that you always have options. When you stop and think about things and listen to your Inner Voice, you can usually clear up some of the confusion. I hope what I've written gives you something to think about. Your email has given me lots to think about and I want to thank you for that.

In friendship,
Terra

UPDATE: The girl wrote back two days after my apology and thanked me for my help. She also wanted to let me know that her "problem" was resolved. So I guess it worked out well. I was grateful for what I learned from the interaction. I forgave myself for rushing to judgment and used it as an opportunity to take another crack at doing the right thing. The next time you're in a situation like this with your kids, hopefully my bad will help you do good.

REAL WORLD ASSIGNMENT:
Second Chances

Not even the Olympic Gold Medalists in parenting get it right every time, so why should we expect to be perfect? We have messed up before and we'll do it again. When it happens and we apologize to our children, we teach them about respect, compassion, and forgiveness. We also let them know that we are doing our best to be good people. When we hang in there, without letting guilt, or the shame from past mistakes, inhibit our good intentions, we teach our kids that they are precious to us and so is our relationship with them.

Listening In—In our desire to help our kids succeed, we parents sometimes imagine that it's our job is to "fix" what's "wrong" with them. In this podcast (AnnieFox.com/podcast/FC003.mp3), I talk about celebrating our kids for exactly who they are with journalist Joan Ryan, author of *The Water Giver: The Story of a Mother, a Son, and Their Second Chance* (Simon and Schuster, 2009).

Fuel for Thought—Recall a time you tried to help someone, but, for whatever reason, you didn't get it right the first time. How did you feel? If you didn't try again, what held you back? If, right now, you got a chance to redo a past misstep with someone, what would you do differently?

Conversations That Count—Talk to your child about "second chances." Share a time when someone gave each of you a second chance. What happened? Recall a time when you didn't give someone a second chance or you didn't give yourself one. What was in the way?

Teach—Make a family agreement that when we fail on our first try, we will credit good intentions and forgive misunderstandings. We will try to graciously give each other second chances and take for ourselves the opportunities we need to learn to be good people. Check in with each other and report your progress.

WHAT WOULD YOU TEACH HERE?

I am a co-leader on a school team. Yesterday, a guy who already graduated said rude things to me in front of everyone. He talked about my poor leadership and how I use humor to hurt people. I admit my sense of humor is fairly sarcastic, but I try to make it is obvious when I am kidding. I'm still very hurt by his remarks. Am I supposed to apologize to him? To the team? I plan on talking to my co-leaders about this but I want to know if I'm in the wrong. I know there is a life lesson in here about learning when and where certain types of humor are appropriate, however I still feel like this guy was in the wrong. —16-year-old

Read my reply (AA 4.3)

———————————

YOU EMBARRASS ME

Even though we know better, parents can lose it big time when we're defied, ignored, or mocked by our children. In a thoughtless fury of frustration we might lash out.

"How dare you talk to your mother/father that way! I've had it with you! You are just a kid and you *will* show me respect!"

That will teach him. That will teach her. Yep, sure will, but what we're teaching has nothing to do with respect. You've probably had an ongoing conversation with your child about the need to be respectful, responsible and mature, but in a split second you've demonstrated none of the above.

Young children are totally dependent on our goodwill, so they seek our approval. We are their heroes and they shower us with affection. Then they grow into teenagers and are always ready to criticize us. That's part of how they establish an independent identity. It may not be comfortable for us, but it is a normal, healthy process for them. (Take some comfort knowing that their hypercritical attitude of us may reflect their general dissatisfaction with themselves.)

When our son was 13 we had this exchange:

> "Come to the movies with us. You don't have any
> other plans and you can pick the film."
> "No thanks."
> "Why not?"
> "Because you embarrass me."
> "In what way?"
> "Mom, everything about you embarrasses me."
> (Oooh! That hurt!)

I could say that I had the self-control not to take his zinger personally, but I'd be lying. You bet I took it personally! (Rereading his words all these years later, I can still remember the sting.) But I didn't attack my son for his "lack of respect." I didn't insult him. I didn't try to guilt trip him for what he said to me. I also didn't turn away from him. His fear of embarrassment had nothing to do with me, not in any profound sense. It had to do with his insecurity and dread that while out with us he might run into a classmate who would undoubtedly think, "What a loser! He has nothing better to do than go out with his parents!"

For the next two years, every time David and I went out to dinner or a movie, we invited our son to join us. And he always turned us down. Many middle school parents report this same pattern. Many young teens would rather be home alone than risk being seen with parents in public (especially on a Friday or Saturday night).

We continued to show our son how much we loved and admired him. We let him know that we appreciated his value as a human being (aside from being our son). Over time, our consistently cheery invitations in the face of repeated cold rejection earned us his respect. If we had belittled him or shown that we weren't confident in his ability to work through this lonely time on his own, we might have missed an opportunity to help him gain self-respect.

As our son matured he became more self-confident and less concerned about how others judged him. He has also become one of the most nonjudgmental people I've ever known. As for feeling embarrassed, our guy loves to perform comedy improv. No fear of embarrassment left in him.

———————

REAL WORLD ASSIGNMENT:
Embarrassment

As our kids grow hungrier for peer approval their tolerance for being embarrassed goes way down. Most tweens would do anything to avoid being made fun of. Which is exactly why, in the T(w)een Popularity Games, teasing and public humiliation are weapons of choice. Teaching our kids to respect others includes our treating *them* with respect.

Fuel for Thought—Recall a funny family story about your child, which you've repeated (often) despite knowing how the story embarrasses him/her. Why do you keep telling it? When we knowingly disregard people's feelings and proceed with our "entertainment," we are being disrespectful and yes, even a bit cruel. To what degree has affectionate teasing gotten out of hand in your family?

Conversations That Count—Talk with your child about the emotion of embarrassment and how uncomfortable it can be. We can't necessarily control what we feel, but we can learn to control how we react. Stopping and thinking before we speak (or text) can help us avoid embarrassing others and ourselves. Encourage your son/daughter to pause and ponder: *If someone said/sent this to me, would I be OK with it? If I wouldn't like it, I won't do it.* Helping them put themselves in someone else's shoes helps nurture feelings of empathy. Acknowledge that it isn't always easy to watch what we say, especially when we're upset or feel pressure to impress. But considering the feelings of others is part of what it takes to be a good person. So we have to practice . . . a lot.

Teach—The next time you hear your kids tease each other, intervene and stop it. Tell them that you are no longer willing for them to be cruel. If they're using put-downs and "jokes," help them get to the bottom of whatever's going on. Make sure no adult in your family (including you) talks to anyone disrespectfully, even as a "joke." If you overhear your child going down that road with a friend, wait until after the friend leaves and talk to your child about the level of disrespect you just witnessed. (Do not embarrass your child in front of a friend!) Say: "Real friends don't talk to each other that way. What's going on with you guys?" Then close your mouth and respectfully *listen* to what your child has to say. Guide him/her in the direction of raising the bar in that friendship.

WHAT WOULD YOU TEACH HERE?

Me and my 13-year-old brother got into a fight at a fast food place. We threw ketchup at each other. Some got on a woman's clothes, and my mom reimbursed her $45. My mom freaked and called us immature babies. She told us she'd get us pacifiers, diapers, and a playpen. My brother started it! Now she's not letting me take drivers ed. She said babies don't get to do grown-up things. Don't I have a right to drive? Can I turn her in for abuse or slander? Can't they make her be a better mom? —15-year-old

Read my reply (AA 4.4)

103

5: HOW CAN I MAKE IT BETTER?

MODELING COMPASSION TO TEACH KINDNESS

"Compassion is not religious business, it is human business. It is not luxury, it is essential for our own peace and mental stability. It is essential for human survival."

—The XIVth Dalai Lama, Tenzin Gyatso

Making things better by alleviating suffering (worry, rage, sadness, fear) may not be Life's only objective, but it's a major opportunity for us while we're here. The adult world is so horribly divided by opinions and viewpoints. Our kids also inhabit real and virtual landscapes where many of their social connections are peppered with conflict dramas in which the players are often required to disregard the feelings of others. That's a problem for them and for all of us. If we don't consciously choose to make positive connections with other people, we know where this is headed. It's headed there already. Teaching our kids to be good people includes helping them develop compassion. When we provide the next generation with peacemaking tools and the social courage to use them, our kids will help heal the world starting with their own (real and virtual) corner of it.

MAYBE WE'RE TEACHING THEM SOMETHING ELSE

A master educator once pointed out to a group of student teachers: "If you're not modeling what you teach, then you're teaching something else." In plain English, that means, if the way you live your life doesn't reflect the values you say you value, then your kids (who are always watching and taking notes) are likely to reject "Be nice" messages and take their lessons from your direct example.

Peer harassment and indifference to suffering are systemic. Put-downs, gossip, and snarkiness are all pretty much the air we breathe. Yet when we see or read about mean-kid behavior, we're righteously stunned. "They tormented that poor girl so relentlessly she committed suicide!? Then the perpetrators actually posted more vicious comments on the victim's Facebook memorial page!!! What is wrong with these kids?!"

What, indeed?

Consider what passes for entertainment, political debate, and adult bonding around the water cooler, in the teacher's lounge, in the blogosphere, and in social media. *We all gossip. It's what people do.* We make jokes at the expense of others. Sometimes the talk is harmless. Sometimes, not so much. If that's the nature of the beasts we are, why feel shocked when our kids' behavior reflects our own? Personally, I find it more surprising when a seventh or eighth grader in our Culture of Cruelty consistently demonstrates sensitivity and kindness. I know that's a harsh statement and believe me when I say it hurts to speak the truth about this. It's uncomfortable to think that the enemy is us . . . but we all need to own it because until we do, we continue to fuel the problem without even knowing it. And any attempts to minimize the prevalence of school bullying or to infer that peer harassment is just "kids being kids" blows another opportunity to turn the ship around.

In my garden, blackberry vines have rooted amongst my rose bushes. I never planted them. Must have sprung up from some bird's deposit. But who cares how they got there? They've now made themselves at home. If my only response is to curse them or try to convince myself that they're not really that bad, those creepers will just laugh and crowd out everything else. But if I really want to be rid of the blackberries, forever, I've get down on my hands and knees, brave those wicked thorns and dig out those suckers by their damn roots.

Same approach applies to bullying. Not only are we parents and teachers responsible for rooting out malevolent student behavior whenever we see it, hear about it, or sense it, we are also morally obligated to watch our own mouths and attitudes . . . all the time. Otherwise "Respect, Compassion, and Social Responsibility" is just a pleasant school motto and the dirty truth is that we're teaching our kids something else.

REAL WORLD ASSIGNMENT:
Walking the Walk

Modeling is our most effective teaching tool, especially when it comes to instilling lessons of compassion. We fail as our kids' teachers when we consistently pass up opportunities to teach them that kindness is cool.

Listening In—Most schools ineffectively deal with peer harassment. In this podcast (AnnieFox.com/podcast/ FC018.mp3), I talk with Dr. Elizabeth J. Meyer, Ph.D., author of *Gender, Bullying, and Harassment: Strategies to End Sexism and Homophobia in Schools* (Teachers College Press, 2009).

Fuel for Thought—That nutty 20th century parenting adage "Do as I say, not as I do" is no way to teach kids to be good people. It only succeeds in teaching kids that rules for treating people with compassion and respect aren't always worth bothering with. In what ways have you demonstrated compassion in the past week? In what ways have others been compassionate toward you? If you can't recall any recent incidents when you intentionally tried to alleviate someone's suffering, set a goal for tomorrow to act with more compassion. At the end of the day, reflect on what happened and how you felt.

Conversations That Count—Discuss the term "mixed messages" with your child. For example, professing that something is important but then acting in a way which reflects indifference. Brainstorm examples of a recent mixed message you and your child may have received or sent. Talk about how it feels when we're saying or doing something that doesn't match the kind of person we think we are. Ask your child to recall a time when s/he felt that you were sending mixed messages. Add your own recent recollections of times when what you did (or failed to do) may have canceled out the lesson you want to teach your child. Be honest!

Teach—Agree, as a family, to call each other out (gently) when we send mixed messages with our words, our silence, our actions or inactions. If the prospect of our children holding us to the same high standard of behavior to which we hold them makes us feel uncomfortable, sorry but there's no way around it. Not if we're sincere about being an exemplary teacher who leads children in the direction of personal ethics and integrity.

WHAT WOULD YOU TEACH HERE?

When I'm with my friends I don't behave. And even though I don't want to act cool and kinda mean, I have no other choice! I don't wanna be with them any more. But if I leave to be with nicer girls, they'll call me names like "You're a user." HELP! —10-year-old

Read my reply (AA 5.1)

——————————————

I DON'T WANT A NEW BABY!

I don't usually write about the challenges of parenting young children, but I made an exception because some of the earliest lessons we teach kids about compassion are in the way we respond to an older child's struggles accepting a younger sibling. So many positive teaching opportunities jumped out at me in this email from a young dad that I wanted to share it.

This man and his wife recently had a second baby and they were surprised at their five-year-old daughter's reaction. *"Emma clearly doesn't like receiving less attention and has shown a change in behavior since the baby arrived. Thankfully she hasn't taken it out on her little brother, just directed it towards us."*

It was only six a.m. but Big Sister's reaction was so familiar I skipped my starter cup of Earl Grey and immediately replied:

Hey Worried Dad,

If not classy, your daughter's reaction is classic. During our son's first six months of life, our daughter (also five at the time) was no ray of sunshine. Like your Emma, our girl never directed her resentment toward her brother, but she was obviously pissed at us . . . specifically me. Stands to reason. Five years she's a mega star. Parents, grandparents, hell, even the UPS guys light up when they see her. She starts walking, talking, telling jokes, drawing pictures, and writing stories . . . OMG! Accolades pour in! That's her life until . . . one day Mom and Dad bring home a little blob in a blue blanket and bingo! Glory Days are gone.

From the point of view of Child #1, the arrival of #2 is the emotional equivalent of Husband telling Wife, "Sweetie, I'd like to introduce you to my second wife. Isn't she beautiful? And guess what? She's going to live with us . . . *forever*. I still love you, but you won't be getting as much attention. We won't be doing as much fun stuff together either. You see, my second wife has lots of needs so I'll be focusing on her. When I'm with her, don't interrupt us. If you do, I'll probably get annoyed. I may even yell. Be quiet while she's sleeping. And don't bother me while I'm resting. Even though it looks like the coast is clear and I may be ready to spend time with you, I don't have much extra energy because it's all going to . . . you guessed it, my second wife.

"Why are you crying and carrying on like that? What do you mean you're "not happy" with these changes? You want to know what am *I* going to do about all this? Nothing. I'm thrilled with the situation. If you've got a problem with it then it's *your* problem. Oh, one more thing . . . I expect you to love my new wife as much as I do and share everything you've got with her. And don't forget to smile. That's very important. I want her to feel welcome."

How would you feel if your one-and-only dumped that bombshell on you? OK, I see you're starting to sense that little Emma has a legitimate beef, but don't blame yourself for any of what she's feeling. Incorporating a new baby into the family isn't an easy transition for anyone. So here are some suggestions that might help:

1) Acknowledge to Emma that her feelings of jealousy, resentment, etc., are *totally valid*. Don't make her feel like she's "bad" if she's not thrilled with the baby. While it's OK for her to feel whatever's she's feeling, obviously it's not OK for her to act out aggressively toward the baby or toward you. Let her know that you and Mom get where she's coming

from and then make sure you provide her with plenty of opportunities to express her feelings in responsible, appropriate, creative, and safe ways.

2) Dad, create special one-on-one time with your daughter. You and she deserve a weekly "date" outside the house, just the two of you. It will do wonders for your relationship and her behavior. Same with Mom and Emma. Insist they go off together at least once a week for a couple of hours while you bond with your new son and give Mom a break.

3) Give Emma special "big sister" responsibilities. (No cleaning up or other yucky duties. Only the fun stuff!) Have her read to the baby. Sing to him. Draw pictures for his wall and let her explain the art to him. Show him how to play with his toys. Tell Emma that her brother wants to get to know her. He's curious about and impressed with all the things she can do. He needs his Big Sister to show him so much, including how to be a good friend. Give her the opportunity to be one of his teachers and they will learn to love and appreciate each other.

It sure turned out that way with our little girl and her baby brother.

_____

REAL WORLD ASSIGNMENT:
Taking Someone's Point of View

When children exhibit aggressive behavior, we may be tempted to shut it down without any discussion. We may even berate them for feeling whatever they're feeling. But an angry child is suffering and compassion is about doing our best to alleviate suffering. Show compassion by talking about feelings in safe, open ways. Granted, this takes time and patience when we might not have much of either, but we are their teachers. When we help our kids learn to express resentment, fear, and disappointment *in words*, we gain understanding of their "side of things." When children and adults feel understood, we can calm down and experience love, coming and going.

Fuel for Thought—Recall a time, growing up, when you felt as if your parents just didn't understand what you were going through. Maybe you tried to explain but were met with impatience. Perhaps, you didn't bother explaining because expressing yourself honestly didn't quite feel "safe." Now think about ways you can make it safer for your children to open up, especially when they're upset. When we listen with compassion we can understand someone else's point of view. Once we begin understanding, we're in a much better position to love and to help.

114

Conversations That Count—Talk to your child about what it means to understand where someone is coming from. Ask: "Since our thoughts are private and we all have our own way of experiencing life, how can we ever really understand another person? Why is it important to try?" Now brainstorm ways in which understanding between people might be impaired *vs.* enhanced.

Teach—The next time there's a conflict at home and things start heating up, calm down and help your children see how it takes at least two people to have a conflict vs. "S/he started it and I'm totally innocent." Make it safe to examine how *both people* contributed to the conflict by asking these open-ended questions:

☞ What did you do that might have added to the conflict?

☞ What did you forget to do that might have added to the conflict?

☞ What do you wish you had said or done instead of what you actually did?

☞ What might you do differently next time?

☞ Look at the situation from the other person's point of view. Imagine what s/he is feeling about what happened between you. What would you have said if you were him/her? What would you have done if you were him/her?

Your child will probably feel better after having thought about this from a cooler, more objective perspective. Hopefully s/he learned something positive that will make it easier to deal with conflict the next time it comes up. After the debriefing, tell your child: "You don't have to talk about

115

this with the person you were angry with, but you might want to."

———————————

WHAT WOULD YOU TEACH HERE?

I'm sick of my Mom. Take two minutes ago, when I asked if I could go on a bike ride with my friend and she said, "NO!" I asked her why I couldn't because it was still light, and I said I would be back before dark. She answered, "I don't feel like letting you go out." What's her problem!? —14-year-old

Read my reply (AA 5.2)

IF YOU DON'T COME DOWN BY THE COUNT OF FIVE, YOU WILL BE PEPPER SPRAYED

When I first read the headline in my morning *San Francisco Chronicle*: "$55,000 FOR PEPPER SPRAYING OF CHILD," I honestly didn't get it. Had someone been paid to hurt a child? Was someone offering to pay to have it done?! It made no sense. Then I read the story and realized the headline referred to a lawsuit settlement won by the parents of a seven-year-old against a police officer. Which of course got me wondering what could possibly cause a cop to use a toxic weapon on a second grader.

Apparently, back in June 2010, a seven-year-old special education student from San Mateo, CA (who, according to the story, has "learning difficulties, dyslexia, anxiety disorder, and social-skill problems") perched on an "unsteady" piece of classroom furniture and refused to get down. A classroom aide called the police. (Well, that makes sense.) An officer arrived with a can of pepper spray. (If you're gonna face a second grader you'd better be prepared.) After warning the child that he'd be pepper sprayed if he didn't get down by the count of five, the officer sprayed the kid! According to the filed complaint, the child knew how to count, but had no idea what pepper spray was. (Guess we should now include it in this week's spelling words.)

Was this an isolated incident of a peace officer flipping out in an elementary school? Apparently not. A quick search revealed how, in April of this year, another elementary school student in a special education class was pepper sprayed by police at his Denver school.

The two incidents could easily be lumped together under the heading of Educational Pepper Spraying, but that would be misleading. While all pepper spray is the same, these two cases of child abuse are not.

In the Denver case, the child behaved violently, throwing furniture, wielding a broken piece of board, cursing, and threatening to "kill" his teachers. The police reportedly felt the safety of the teachers and students was threatened, and they needed to subdue that eight-year-old quickly.

In the San Mateo incident, apparently the child was in danger of tumbling from a bookcase and they needed to subdue that seven-year-old quickly. (Though it would seem that a pepper sprayed child is less able to maintain his balance than an unsprayed child, but I digress.)

I wasn't present at either scene, but here's what I'm thinking: If a police officer doesn't have the training and common sense to safely get a seven- or eight-year-old under control, then what the hell is that officer doing on the force? And why is that officer the go-to person to send to a school?

I'm also wondering if this might not be a case of "When all you've got is a can of pepper spray, then everyone looks like a dangerous suspect needing to be subdued quickly." And I'm curious about the lessons the victims and the rest of the students took home that day about police officers and teachers . . . adults who are supposed to care about kids and know how to help them when they're in trouble.

It takes a village, right? Wonder what the parents thought about the rest of the village when they found out what happened in school.

REAL WORLD ASSIGNMENT:
Knowing What's Needed

Parenting and teaching are both highly nuanced arts. Being a good person also requires nuance, which is usually learned in the family. When we take a nuanced approach to helping people, by thoughtfully expressing our perspective, observing, asking questions, listening, understanding, and acting with compassion, we are more likely to be of real service to others.

Fuel for Thought—Sometimes our best intentions miss the mark and only make things worse. Sometimes we don't take time to assess what's really needed, or we make assumptions and end up not being helpful at all. Recall a time when someone's well-meaning response actually made you feel worse. Recall a time when a compassionate, nuanced response was helpful.

Conversations That Count—Talk with your child about the way some people react more intensely than others. Maybe you or someone in your family is like this. Let your child know that this tendency may be part of our in-born temperament and it isn't necessarily a good thing or a bad thing. If your child typically gets very upset when things aren't going well, ask, "When you're feeling that way, how would you like other people to respond so we can help you?" Listen to his/her answer and take note. Conversely, if someone else in the family is easily upset, ask your child, "At those times, how might we be more helpful to _____?"

Teach—Make a family agreement to try harder to understand each other when we are upset. Get into the habit of observing what's going on and focusing on being truly helpful. Instead of making assumptions, let's agree to ask each other, "What can I do to help?" Sometimes, the most helpful response is to hang in there with love and compassion.

———————————

WHAT WOULD YOU TEACH HERE?

Our 15-year-old daughter asked permission to date an 18-year-old. We said no, explaining the maturity gap is too large. She disagreed but appeared to respect our decision. When we found out she'd been seeing the boy anyway, we took away her cell phone and grounded her. We told her once this relationship is over, we'll begin to trust her again, and restore privileges. Did we overreact? How do we get our daughter to understand our perspective and guide her?

—My child's teacher

Read my reply (AA 5.3)

121

ONE FOOT
IN FRONT OF
THE OTHER

I don't believe in Santa's Naughty or Nice List, but I do believe in the inherent value of doing good deeds. I always try, at least in public, to be a positive role model, just in case some child happens to be watching and taking notes. In other words, I do my best to avoid missteps.

Some missteps can be corrected before it's too late. Like when you choose a puny pot for making applesauce. After cutting up and tossing in four apples any fool can see that the other eleven on the counter will never fit into that pot. So you simply dump everything into a larger pot and carry on. Misstep unstepped. That assumes, of course, that a certain someone who already mentioned how the first pot was obviously too small isn't standing right there watching. If he is and you two have been keeping score about such things, then timely self-correction without losing face is more challenging. But it's still a viable and prudent option.

Some missteps, on the other hand, can't be undone. Like making that offhand comment when you knew a certain person probably wasn't going to fully appreciate the humor. Even if you swear you were "Just kidding!" you're still stuck having to apologize and deal with your own disappointment in your lack of self-control. You're also left wondering why the hell you haven't yet learned that everything that pops into your head a) isn't as funny as you think it is and/or b) isn't worth saying.

As I write this, it is now December. 'Tis the season of spreading goodwill and comfort in the cold. So I light candles and look for opportunities to take steps in the right direction. And I got one this afternoon! As David and I walked to the post office, we passed a neighbor standing in front of her house. She wore a thin pink dress, bedroom slippers, and an agitated expression. She said something to us, but since the guy across the street was running his leaf blower, I couldn't make out what it was.

Just so you know, this neighbor is . . . how can I put this . . . a bit erratic. Over the years we've heard her scream at passing cars, "SLOW DOWN!!" And at us, "DID YOU SEE THAT? JUST LETS THE DOG RUN AROUND! NO LEASH! NO SENSE!" Because I never know what I'll get from her, I was a bit apprehensive when I saw her talking to me. At that moment I could easily have begged off by pantomiming something like: "Sorry, I'd love to stop and chat but I can't hear you because the darn leaf blower is too loud. So I'll just shrug and smile and wave and keep on walking."

But that felt like a misstep. And I had the sneaking suspicion the campus rep from Karma College was lurking about taking notes. So I inhaled, exhaled, crossed the street and went up to her.

LADY: Did you see the mailman up the street? Has he come down the hill yet?

ANNIE: I didn't see him, but we already got our mail.

LADY (frowning): So did I. But I wonder if he's passed by yet.

ANNIE: Yeah. I think he's gone for the day.

She looked upset as she stood there in the cold. Her toes were kinda bluish in those flimsy slippers.

ANNIE: Was there something you wanted to mail? Because we're walking to the post office.

Magic words! She lit up and ran into the house. I stood there hoping she wouldn't come out lugging a fifty-pound box and toss me some stamps. But no. She emerged a moment later waving a single white stamped envelope . . . Christmas card-size.

LADY: It's for a man in a nursing home. You'll take it to the post office for me?

ANNIE: Sure thing.

Misstep unstepped. Right foot forward.

REAL WORLD ASSIGNMENT:
Misconceptions Block Understanding

We assume we know so much more about other folks than we actually do. Teaching kids to be good people includes helping them understand how biases get in the way of knowing who people really are, what they need, and how we can help them.

Fuel for Thought—From the We're on this Speck Together file comes some food for thought: "For small creatures such as we, the vastness is bearable only through love." —Carl Sagan. Think back to middle or high school. What did your peers assume about you that wasn't true? How do imagine those assumptions affected people's relationships with you? Think about a former classmate who had a certain "reputation" which led you to have certain assumptions about him/her. How did your assumptions color your behavior toward that person?

Conversations That Count—Talk with your child about the concept of the "judge" within us who rates other people mostly in terms of what we like/admire about them and what we don't. Discuss how unfair it can feel to be judged, especially when the "judges" don't really know us.

Teach—Make a pledge to monitor your "judgmental" thoughts more carefully and try to catch them before they become words. Each time we let the judge put someone down, *She is so* _____. *He is always* _____. *He's weird. She's a bitch.* we stack another brick in the wall of misunderstanding. With less judging, we get to know each other better. Let's teach kids to build bridges, not walls.

––––––––––––––––––––

WHAT WOULD YOU
TEACH HERE?

I like black clothes, which means "gothic" to my mom. She says "those people" are into drugs. I've explained that it's just a style, but she only gets more upset and threatens to lock me in my room. I'm trying to see it from her point of view, and I can kinda understand. She thinks, "I had this sweet little kid, and it's like he's turning into the devil." How do I convince her I'm still me under those bondage pants? It's not going to change my personality or my point of view on certain things. What's the big deal? —16-year-old

Read my reply (AA 5.4)

6: HOW DO YOU THINK THAT MAKES HIM/HER FEEL?

STRETCHING YOUNG MINDS AND HEARTS TO EMPATHIZE

"I hope to leave my children a sense of empathy and pity and a will to right social wrongs"

—Anita Roddick

Stepping back from our own emotions to take in the feelings of others is a lifelong practice. It's challenging because we are, by nature, so egocentric. We want what we want now because we feel what we're feeling now. When we experience intense emotions we don't have a lot of extra bandwidth to think about anyone else. But we need to learn to stretch emotionally because taking into consideration the feelings of others is the key to achieving healthy relationships. Teaching kids to be good people includes helping them understand their own emotions, while assessing the feelings of others and factoring it all into their decision-making.

BROKEN KIDS ARE BREAKING ALL OF US

I remember October 1, 2010. My friend Rachel emailed to find out if I'd blogged yet about the cyberbullying incident that ended in a Rutgers University freshman killing himself. I told her the news had really upset me, but I had no insights that couldn't be found elsewhere. What do you say when yet another teen is so victimized by bullies s/he can't figure out what the hell to do to make things OK again and gives up everything just to end the suffering?

"I'm sitting here crying," I told Rachel. "But I've got nothing to write." The casualness with which these acts of torment are perpetrated absolutely stuns me. But what else is new? So, no. I wasn't going to blog about it.

Then I watched Ellen Degeneres talking about the tragedy. Looking straight at the camera, with obvious emotion, Ellen said, "It's hard enough being a teen and figuring out who you are without people attacking you. There are messages everywhere that validate this kind of bullying and taunting and we have to make it stop." And to the kids watching, she offered, "Things will get easier. People's minds will change and you should be alive to see it."

Still I was not going to blog about what happened to Tyler Clementi and what he did as a result of his roommate's insensitivity. I wasn't going to, even though his death was the fourth in a string of Fall 2010 Welcome Back-to-School cruelties that ended in suicide. It was depressing, but what more could be said?

Then I listened to a radio interview with Justin Patchin of the Cyberbullying Research Center, a clearinghouse of information dedicated to providing information about "the nature, extent, causes, and consequences of cyberbullying amongst adolescents." Patchin told NPR's Melissa Block that when he speaks to teens who use their phones and computers to commit acts of intentional cruelty they "genuinely do not realize that harm could come from it." He went on to say that these kids "don't see it as something wrong." Rather, they think of what they're doing as "fun or funny" and "not that big of a deal."

For real?!! The tormentors don't view this behavior as wrong?! If that's the case then we're looking at a whole lot of kids who are broken in ways that prevent them from thinking beyond the itch of "Hey, I've got a great idea!" So broken that they blithely launch a personally addressed cluster bomb packed with malice and truly believe it's "not a big deal."

With kids like that as our only hope for the future we'd be in deep doodoo. Fortunately, these aren't the only kids out there. There are plenty of teens and adults who aren't buying into the notion that any of this is fun or funny. They're deadly serious about fighting back, supporting each other and changing the Culture of Cruelty for any kid, tween, or teen who's catching flak for being different.

If your son or daughter is gay, lesbian, bisexual, or transgender (or you suspect s/he may be) it's possible s/he is targeted at school and/or online. Put yourself squarely at the center of your child's support network and do whatever it takes to make sure s/he feels your unconditional love and acceptance. Point your child in the direction of the It Gets Better Project (ItGetsBetter.org). And make sure your child is also aware of the awesome online work being done by The Trevor Project. (TheTrevorProject.org). If necessary, advocate for your child at school. And do not hesitate to seek professional counseling if you suspect your child may be depressed or at risk for hurting himself/herself, or someone else.

Now let's address the other side of this issue. Every tormentor is *someone's* child. If you see, hear, or sense that your son/daughter, or any of their friends, is or has been harassing someone, step up and teach them, beyond a shade of a doubt, that this behavior is unacceptable.

I just found out that October is National Bullying Prevention Month, which is cool, but what does that make the other 11 months? Look, no one needs a national campaign to be part of the solution here. It starts at home and continues every day. Teach your children *good*.

Hm. I guess I did have something to write about.

REAL WORLD ASSIGNMENT:
Challenging the Culture of Cruelty

When conversations veer in the direction of: "Those people aren't worthy of respect . . ." we may feel conflicted, but we don't always speak up. If we did, we'd live in a world of fewer personal attacks because that garbage wouldn't be tolerated. Of course, we need to tell kids, "Do the right thing!" but that's not enough of what they need from us. They need our understanding that kids who buck the system pay the price at school and online. One of our primary teaching objectives is helping them learn that US and THEM is a myth. We are all us and cruel's not cool . . . ever.

Listening In—When teens have a falling out with friends, they often resort to aggressive and destructive social behaviors played out in the high stakes indelible world of social media. In this podcast (AnnieFox.com/podcast/FC013.mp3), I talk with Rosalind Wiseman, student empowerment activist and *NY Times* best-selling author of *Queen Bees and Wannabes* (Three Rivers Press, 2009).

Tuning In—Please take two minutes to watch this short video about The Charter for Compassion (youtube.com/watch?v=wktlwCPDd94). Share it with your children. Let it inspire your teaching and their learning.

133

Fuel for Thought—"We are here to awaken from our illusion of separateness." —Thich Nhat Hanh

Try on the notion, if only for a moment, that the differences between us, which we all make so much of, are just an illusion, a fantasy. Breathe in slowly and evenly as you take in the thought: *We are here to awaken from our illusion of separateness.* Then, as you slowly exhale, think: *I open my heart and connect to my family and all people with love.* If we made it a top priority to connect through our shared humanity instead of sniping over differences, how might that affect the way we live life and the way we teach our children?

Conversations That Count—Ask your child: "How do you define 'mean' behavior? Recall a time when someone was mean to you. Recall a time when you were mean to someone." Talk about kids using social media to be mean. If you hear something unsettling, stay calm (breathe) so the conversation can continue safely. Show that you understand how complex your child's friendship issues can be and how easily one can lose control and end up doing things we later regret. Ask your son/daughter: "Why do you think it might be easier for some people to be mean via text or computer than face-to-face?" Another question worth asking and answering: "When someone is mean to you, what are willing to do? Where do you draw the line?"

Teach—Brainstorm a set of family guidelines for behavior online and off. It's all about respect. Make cruelty in any form, unacceptable in your family. Teach your child practical ways to manage destructive feelings, without lashing out online or off. Please read my Parent's Pledge to Raise a Good Digital Citizen (QT 6.1) for a reality check and some helpful tips.

WHAT WOULD YOU TEACH HERE?

I'm a really sensitive guy. Everyone says I'm a sissy. People say, "Don't talk like that" and "Don't sit like that." People have turned away from me since I was 10. My little sister is eight. My parents are so rude to her. I can see in her eyes she's lonely without friends to play with. Even if it's stupid, I feel that pain. I don't want her to suffer the same fate as me. I can't stop feeling sad for her, and I can't stand watching someone really small feeling pain. —15-year-old

Read my reply (AA 6.1)

HITTING DAD!?

While Dad ordered lunch at the food court, his five-year-old son laughed and repeatedly hit him. I watched, wrestling with my inner Butt-insky and wondered what was going on. The kid might have been hungry, but that didn't seem to explain his extreme behavior. I mean Dad was in the process of getting him food . . . fast food. I know some kids have zero tolerance to stomach rumblings and waiting, but this little guy didn't seem angry or frustrated. Was there some unseen challenge contributing to this child's aggression? Could be. No way I could tell for sure. And if that were the case, I would be totally out of line judging him or his father's parenting skills. But let's just say, for argument's sake, that this child was neurotypical, and that he was enjoying this "fight" as much as he seemed to be. Where might he have learned to derive such pleasure from clobbering Dad? That's easy—from Dad himself. Here's how today's lesson went:

Junior starts swinging and Dad totally tunes out the behavior. Or pretends to. Of course, the boy turns up the volume because being ignored drives kids up the wall. The assault continues to a point where Dad can no longer speak intelligibly to the woman behind the counter. He then turns to his son with a smile and a chuckle and says, "Now you stop that." What happens next? The kid giggles and punches Dad in the gut.

By now I'm *this* close to inserting myself into a family affair, when Dad, noticing the glares of several adults, grips both of the boy's hands in one of his own and flashes a phony angry face. Junior hoots with joy and kicks Dad in the shin! Without so much as an "Ow," Doormat Dad smiles weakly at the server and completes the lunch order.

We've all seen public displays of a parent's wrong-headed response to a child's behavior. We've all had self-righteous thoughts that run the route of "Why are you letting your four-year-old disrespect you? Are you nuts? Teach her that whining doesn't work and that no means no."

Obviously "I said no" won't get every kid's attention, even when we actually mean it. I also realize that the Bad Parent Police frequently rush to condemn good parents, when the kids are not neurotypical (despite how they look). I'm guessing you are a good parent. You've probably read more than one parenting book. And somewhere you may have picked up this advice: "Ignore the behavior you want less of and reinforce with praise the behavior you want more of."

Generally speaking, it's not a bad strategy. Choosing to stay calmly assertive when our kids are being disrespectful keeps our emotions in check so we can think more clearly and parent more effectively. When we model self-control we teach our children that mature adults know how to be caring and rational even when someone pushes our buttons. Granted, this is much easier read than done. But we can all see that Doormat Dad's strategy first to ignore his child's aggression and then to reward it with smiles and joking, broadcasts a bankrupt message: "I accept your behavior, and you have permission to treat me like crap." Teach that, and we may damage our child's ability to develop respect and empathy for others.

I'm no expert in behavior modification. And this isn't a book about discipline. It's a resource for teaching kids to be good people. So here's a tip: When our kids hurt us or others, and we fail to tell them the truth, we miss an opportunity to help them understand that the universe does not end at their fingertips. Being a good person requires taking the point of view of someone whose shin is on the receiving end of your kick. If we don't tell our kids clearly and without joking, "OW! Stop! That hurts!" when it does, then we're teaching them they can do whatever they damn please and needn't bother to stop and consider how their choices might impact others. Which, come to think of it, is the antithesis of empathy. Without empathy, none of us can create and maintain healthy relationships. When we accept unacceptable behavior, the takeaway will come back to bite, punch, or kick us again and again.

REAL WORLD ASSIGNMENT:
Respect

Respect is the foundation of all healthy adult relationships. Along with unconditional love, respect is also the essence of our relationship with our kids. When our interactions with children come from a respectful place, we teach them that all people (even very young ones) deserve respect. Treat them with respect and kids are also likely to learn that respect is a two-way street.

Fuel for Thought—Think about how you and your parents showed respect for each other. Recall the ways people in your birth family did not treat each other respectfully. Now think about what respect looks like in your relationship with your child(ren) and in the sibling relationships your kids have with each other. What adjustments (if any) would you like to make?

Conversations That Count—We often use the word *respect* to teach kids about kindness and social responsibility. We assume they understand it the same way we do. To make sure you and your children are on the same page, talk about what respect means. Put your heads together to define it. *Listen more than you talk*. Working at a keyboard makes it easier since there may be a bit of word crafting until you both agree on a definition. Once you have a working definition, talk about what respect actually looks like in the real world. Share day-to-day examples that occur at home and at school. Listen respectfully to your child's ideas.

Teach—Work with everyone in the family to create a set of clear ground rules that reflect the level of mutual respect you want in your family. Talk about whether the same rules apply to everyone. If not, why not? Remember, a family isn't a democracy. Everyone doesn't have equal power to make decisions. Parents need to be leaders and kids are most cooperative when they feel they are being treated fairly and respectfully.

WHAT WOULD YOU TEACH HERE?

My 14-year-old has no problems at school and her friends' parents say she is a dream to be around! But she responds to her dad and me as if everything we say is stupid or embarrassing. I'd rather not talk to her at all sometimes. We've told her this is unacceptable, and she improves for a short time, then goes right back to her sharp speaking ways. It's almost as if she cannot control herself. How can we help her learn to speak to us more respectfully so that we too, can enjoy our daughter? —My child's teacher

Read my reply (AA 6.2)

GOOD DOG
AND THE
META-MESSAGE

I had the pleasure of interviewing Rachel Simmons the Wise for my podcast series. We talked about her book *The Curse of the Good Girl: Raising Authentic Girls with Courage and Confidence*. We also discussed how often parents engage in meta-conversations with their children (i.e., parent says one thing and an unspoken message churns just below the surface). With all that doublespeak, how can a teen learn to be authentic and express the truth of her heart? Not very easily. And it isn't just parents and daughters. As Rachel put it, no matter who you're talking to or what relationship you've got, "there's always a meta-conversation going on."

For example:

Parent: Oh, you're still playing that game.
Meta-message: I just know you won't get your homework done tonight and then what? You think I like being on your case? Well, I don't! But if I don't keep after you how are you ever going to get into a decent college?
Mini meta-message: You're lazy and I'm disappointed in you.

Parent: Don't you think your other jeans would look better with that top?
Meta-message: Those jeans are too tight and too low cut. They make you look fat and slutty. What will Grandma say when she sees you wearing that? She's going to think I'm a terrible mother to let you dress that way!
Mini meta-message: You're fat and you embarrass me.

Parent: How's your buddy Ryan these days?

Meta-message: Are you two still friends? Did something happen between you? Are you now hanging out with people I should be worried about? (Sigh) You and I used to be able to talk about stuff. Now you don't tell me anything. What else are you hiding from me? Maybe I don't even want to know!

Mini meta-message: You're not a good friend.

I've been thinking about meta-messages and how I use them. Whether they're conscious or not, communication patterns between people often determine who we like to hang out with and who doesn't make our "favorites" list.

Early one morning my dog, Josie, and I snuck out of the house before anyone was up. We headed for the nearby hills, and because Josie was still full of puppy beans and needed her off-leash time. She instantly vanished through the trees tracking deer and squirrels and nosing the underbrush for ticks thumbing a ride. While she was gone I walked on, enjoying the quiet light and the colors. Every so often I'd whistle for Josie, and she'd reappear, sometimes from behind me on the trail, sometimes from way ahead. We'd smile at each other and wag our tails. "Yes! Good dog!" Then I'd give her a treat. After each reunion she'd take off again, and I continued hiking.

So it went for about an hour. When I finally put her back on leash I thought about my meta-conversation with Josie and why she happily kept returning to me. The way I figure, it comes down to this . . . each of us, dog and human, prefers to hang with those who tell us we are good dogs.

It also helps if they give us treats.

———————

REAL WORLD ASSIGNMENT:
The Meta-Message

We constantly interact with our family and the feelings we develop for each other, over time, come from a series of teeny mini-messages. Some of these messages are loving, caring, empathetic. Some are dismissive, aggressive, and disrespectful. Our feelings for anyone with whom we have a long-term relationship are a balance of all those overt and covert messages. Teaching kids to be good people requires being real, for sure, but it also requires our being kind to them so that they, in turn can learn kindness and acceptance.

Fuel for Thought—"People will forget what you said, people will forget what you did, but people will never forget how you made them feel." —Maya Angelou

Think about the relationship you had with each of your parents, grandparents, siblings, cousins, and other members of your family. What's the overall feeling you have toward each person? Do you smile when they come to mind, or do you feel something else? Think about how you learned to feel this way about these important people in your life. Their behavior toward *you* shaped it! What long-term feelings are you helping to shape in the hearts, minds, and emotional memories of your children?

Conversations That Count—Kids are often unequivocal about whether they like or dislike someone and they are not shy about letting people know. Say: "Before you knew _____ (name of a friend or ex-friend) you didn't have any feelings about him/her. So, where did your current feelings come from?" Explain how relationships can grow over time and how we can, by the way we respond, move a relationship in a respectful, caring direction, or in the opposite direction. Being a good person involves the intention to create and maintain positive connections with other people.

Teach—Think about a relationship that could use some TLC —maybe it's the one you and your child have with each other . . . or one that you each have with someone else. Brainstorm ways you could make that relationship a healthier, more trustworthy, respectful, caring one. Create some concrete action steps. Set daily or weekly goals. Be accountable to each other with progress reports.

———————————

WHAT WOULD YOU TEACH HERE?

What do you do if your friend is bullying you and you don't want to hurt them? —11-year-old

Read my reply (AA 6.3)

_____

OF COURSE, I'M LISTENING. WHAT DID YOU SAY?

Good ol' Mr. Rogers knew what he was talking about when he carefully put on sneakers and sweater and sang: "I mean I just might make mistakes if I should have to hurry up and so I like to take my time." To his credit, that guy could really focus on one thing at a time. I know nothing about his off-camera life, but I'd like to imagine that when he was home, Fred Roger's own children got even more attention than his shoelaces.

Recently I've become aware of how cranky, stressed, and distracted I get when trying to do a whole lot of stuff at once. So I'm trying to slow down and zero in. But it ain't easy. Admittedly, as I am writing this, I'm also picking remnants of toasted almonds out of my teeth, answering email, tweeting, and squinting at the screen wondering how much longer it will take for the eyeglasses I left in our hotel room in Elko, NV, to make their way home. (Soon please!)

Tweens and teens constantly email me for advice. They say their parents "don't listen." Parents say the same about teens. We'd all like to improve parent-teen communication so we can feel bonded to each other, but that's not going to happen when we're busy with six other things—or even one other thing.

Obviously we can't always drop everything to listen to our children. But let's be honest: not many of us perform open heart surgery or negotiate international crises from home. So when our kids want to talk, *need* to talk, we could take a break, unplug, and focus on them if we choose to. But most of the time we keep doing whatever we're doing and shift into unconscious distracted listening ("Uh, huh. Uh, huh.").

Here's why distracted listening is a bad habit:

☞ **It's disrespectful.** In a healthy relationship, respect, and empathy flow in both directions. We want our kids' respect. We want them to care enough about what we're saying so they will really listen and understand where we're coming from. That's why we've got to show them the same respect . . . more often than not.

☞ **It's not fooling them.** Even toddlers have been known to put their chubby little hands on the face of Mom or Dad to get a parent's attention. If an 18-month-old knows that no eye contact means we're preoccupied, how can we hope to fake it with a teen? And why would we want to try? During this fleeting phase of their lives they're becoming young adults. Their thoughts and feelings are important to them and they ought to be important to us. Tune in all the way and we can better understand their changes. That will lead to more empathy for their struggles and more opportunities to influence them in the right direction.

☞ **It makes them think we don't care.** When we are distracted instead of focused on listening, we're showing our kids that "other things" are more important than they are. We don't really feel that way so way send that message? There is no one else in our child's life that ever gives 100 percent attention. Let him/her at least get it from us while we're having a conversation.

☞ **It's lousy modeling.** Our kids don't listen to us because a) sometimes they need to pretend to shut us out so they can build their own identity and b) we haven't been

147

showing them what empathetic, active listening looks and feels like. We can't do much about their developmental need to shut us out at times, but by making a conscious effort to listen well (with eye contact, 100 percent of our attention, and an open heart and mind), we teach them to listen more attentively to us and to the other people in their lives. In fact, kids whose parents model empathetic listening are often the most empathetic kids. Need proof? Just watch them interact with their friends, especially when those friends need a real friend.

Caveat! Don't assume sincere efforts to regularly unplug from technology and tune-in to the real world Empathy Channel will rid the family of all disharmonies. (We're working on improved communication here, not miracles.) But if we focus more, our kids will feel that we're trying harder to understand them and there will be positive ripples. Including less confusion about what was actually said in a conversation. That means less arguments studded with gems like: "I never said that!" "You never said that!" and "What are you talking about?!"

That'd be cool, right? Hello? Hello? Anyone listening?

REAL WORLD ASSIGNMENT:
Focus

While we're all moving in ten directions at once, online and off, the notion of evenings and weekends where parents and kids spend unplugged time together is laughably retro. But we've got to create an antidote to 21st century craziness because life is neither virtual nor infinite. Listening (the old-fashioned way) with open eyes, mind, and heart is the best way we connect with our kids and teach them how to connect with others. That's what we want from them and for them. Friends aren't just on Facebook and Twitter, they're right here in the real world and they deserve our attention when we're with them.

Fuel for Thought—Think about a relationship in which the other person is often "distracted." What is it like being with him/her? Contrast that with someone who is normally "there" with you. Now think about the level of "there-ness" you give to your family. If you could do a better job focusing on your children/partner/parents, set a goal for the next week: Be with your family when you're with them. Do not allow distractions to get in the way. Observe what happens.

Conversations That Count—Talk with your child about digital distractions, including phones, games, TV shows, and computers. Ask her/him to rate the family (on a 1–10 scale) regarding the presence of distractions while people are talking to each other. (Scoring scale: 1 = When we talk to each other, we're not doing anything else; 10 = When we talk to each other there's always a "distraction" present.) Your 21st century child may not even have noticed or considered these distractions as anything other than "normal." Ask what s/he thinks family life (*vis-à-vis* "distractions") might look like when s/he's grown up.

Teach—Create an Unplugging challenge. Start small and make it fun! For example, "On Saturday from 4:00–5:00 p.m. we're unplugging for an hour." You will probably get pushback from tweens/teens. The more resistance, the more likely they have a *connection addiction*. But don't cave in. Be upbeat. Remind them it's only for one hour. Then take suggestions for a non-tech activity the family can do together for that short time. Play a board game, card game, make popcorn, build something, cook something, bake something, create something, take a walk, go for a bike ride, have an impromptu meal outside, read aloud from a mystery book, look at old family photos and tell stories. Etc. etc. Be together. Focus on each other. Have fun. Repeat often.

———————

WHAT WOULD YOU TEACH HERE?

My boyfriend just broke up with me online. How irritating! It hurt me a lot that he didn't care about my feelings. He says we don't spend enough time together, and never really connected. We both have busy schedules. I try to make time for him. He never seems to hold up his end of the bargain. I try to have conversations but blows me off to play computer games with his friends. The hardest part is that I still care for him and want to be with him. What should I do? Is it worth pursuing? —16-year-old

Read my reply (AA 6.4)

7: HOW ABOUT ME?!

SEEING BEYOND
LIKES AND DISLIKES
TO THE BIGGER PICTURE

"Is the glass half empty, half full, or twice as large as it needs to be?"

—Author Unknown

At the beginning of life we have no awareness of anything beyond ME and MY NEEDS. But as we grow, our parents, our teachers, our peers, help us expand that micro view. Teaching kids to be good people includes helping them realize that beyond our own fingertips, beyond our immediate desires, is a world filled with people whose needs and emotions are as important as ours. We are part of the same "whole" that they are. That's the Bigger Picture our kids need in their viewfinders as we help them develop social problem-solving skills.

THAT'S BETTER THAN THIS . . . OR IS IT?

Have you ever gotten up close and personal with a lemon tree and noticed how cool they are? I hadn't until I moved to California. Now I've got my own dwarf Meyer lemon and let me tell you that tree is an underrated miracle of nature. Right now, it's got teeny flower buds, heavenly smelling blossoms, baby green fruit, and ripe golden orbs, all at the same time! On a cosmic level, the lemon tree always manifests its entire life cycle, simultaneous living its past, present, and future! How cool is that?

One might assume straddling the time-space continuum causes internal conflict for the tree. Like maybe an undeveloped puny green guy eyes a juicy yellow beauty and gripes, "Damn! How come I'm not more mature?" Or some blossom whose petals flap in the wind, whines about how unfair it is that she's no longer taut and firm like that sweet young bud over there. But noooo. The tree has evolved to a point where no phase of life is any better or worse than any other. In the realm of lemon trees, there are no complaints, only total acceptance. What is, is. Lemon embraces all of it with equal acceptance and grace.

We humans on the other hand are hardwired for complaining. Even (maybe especially) those of us who have pretty soft lives compared to most others on the planet. Adults often evaluate things in terms of what's "wrong." So how surprising is it that our kids frequently complain? Especially older kids, because as they get older we're more likely to find fault in what *they* do or fail to do! In addition to what we're teaching them through negative modeling, teens are already incredibly judgmental. After all, they're grappling with some key questions: *Am I cool enough? Am I hot enough? Am I good enough?* The less confident they feel (from the feedback we and their "friends" pile on and from their own self-doubt), the more likely they are to complain. The more they complain, the more we complain about *them*.

Just so you don't misunderstand, I'm not advocating an all-Zen-all-the-time approach to living, where we make damn sure we never find fault with anything. That's too tough to be practical. Besides there are certain situations that are inherently faulty! Like when the cottage cheese has gone off. No amount of Ohmmming is going to make me smile when I lift that lid and get a whiff. So yeah, life serves up plenty of unacceptable tidbits. When you've got one, just DO SOMETHING about it. Complaining is never a prerequisite for action. Nor is it a substitute.

When a family member presents us with something unacceptable, rather than exploding and losing control of mind and mouth, try this instead: "This cell phone bill of $1,000 is unacceptable. You will pay this, not me." That's not a complaint. That's a simple directive. When we whine less, and fill our sentences with more verbs (calls to action), we might get more cooperation and less complaining from our kids. At the same time, we are teaching them that a positive attitude helps us deal with life's inconveniences more effectively than complaints.

On that positive note, I want to report that last week I picked all the ripe lemons from the tree and made lemon marmalade. Not to complain or anything, either the recipe was wrong, or I misread it. Either way, the results were . . . uh . . . not edible. Fortunately the tree's still got plenty of green babies. In another month or so, I'll take another shot at it.

REAL WORLD ASSIGNMENT:
Complaining vs. Making It Better

There is an important concept at the foundation of Jewish tradition known as *Tikkun olam* (repairing the world). The concept refers to going out of one's way to make things better for others. Good people are doers, repairers of the world. Complainers have a lot of negative things to say, but they are rarely people of positive action. Making our children more aware of complaining vs. helping, encourages them to do good.

156

Fuel for Thought—When you feel something isn't OK, how do you usually respond? Are you more likely to take direct action or complain? Think about the people you've known who were "complainers"? What was it like to be around those people? How was/is your mood and attitude affected by being around a complainer vs. someone who addresses problems with a positive attitude?

Conversations That Count—Talk with your child about the amount of complaining in the family. (No need to single out any individual, because we all do it at times.) Some complaints point to things can be changed. ("It's too hot in here!" "We're out of toothpaste again!") But most complaints aren't helpful because they refer to situations that can't be changed. ("This math assignment is too long!" "Why did I get her for a sister?") Ask your child to "play back" complaints s/he regularly hears from you. Then you play back complaints you regularly hear from your child. How much of the grumbling and whining amongst family members has become a bad habit with no real intention toward making things better? What might the family do about that?

Teach—Assuming everyone wants less complaining/nagging, challenge each member of the family to catch himself/herself (not anyone else) in the act of complaining. Instead of complaining about someone or something:

a) Communicate directly about what needs to be done.
b) Skip the complaining, and do some or all of what needs to be done (on your own).
c) Change what you *can* change, and change your attitude about the rest.

Report back in a week about the progress the whole family has made in creating a more positive atmosphere.

WHAT WOULD YOU TEACH HERE?

My 12-year-old son stayed with my parents for a few days along with his cousins. He complained that Grandma likes his cousins more than him. My mom said a cousin tried to see my son's book and she told him, "Let him. It's not a big deal." My son requested to be picked up early. I don't discount my son's feeling towards his cousins, but I said he needed to stay and work things out. I also felt the situation was an opportunity for growth. I'm concerned that he always jumps to feeling like the victim. —My child's teacher

Read my reply (AA 7.1)

GIVING ATTITUDE VS. AN ATTITUDE OF GIVING

For the first few years of life kids aren't especially capable of telling people exactly what they want. Which is why helpful, loving parents and grandparents who want to keep the little ones happy, pepper them with questions that often begin with: "Do you want _____?" Since we're not yet ready for conversation, the grownups fill in the blank:

> Do you want to play with this?
> Do you want a story?
> Do you want to go to the park?
> Do you want Mint Chip or Jamoca Almond Fudge?

Our every wish becomes our parents' command. That's why we quickly we learn to say "*I want _____.*" Being a little kid is such sweet gig!

Then comes the day when a parent says, "NO" to one of our demands, and our old brain explodes. "What did you say?! What do you *mean* it's too close to dinner? What do you *mean* it costs too much and you won't buy it for me? This is outrageous!!" We don't have all those words, so we reiterate the obvious for stupid Mommy/Daddy, "*BUT I WANT IT!!!!!*"

The tantrums don't always work, but they work sometimes and for little humans that's just enough reinforcement to keep hope and self-centeredness alive.

At around age three, as we become more aware of the power dynamics within our family, we start testing boundaries. That's the time a parent's "Do you want _____?" may take on a sinister ring:

Do you want me to take that away from you?
Do you want a time out?
Do you want me to tell Daddy?
Do you want me to give you something to cry about?

This last rhetorical question was surprisingly popular amongst certain parents during the second half of the last century. Hopefully it's gone the way of the landline, but I've got no empirical data either way.

Obviously all those years of "Do you want _____?" congeal in the spongy language and reward centers of our brain where we realize how important our happiness is to Mom and Dad. Because we are all about making it easy for them to please us, we learn to be very specific with our demands and why they ought to be met . . . NOW:

"I want _____. *And yes, I am old enough!*"
"I want _____. *'Cause I'm the only one who doesn't have one!*"
"I want a new _____. *'Cause my old one sucks!*"
"I want you to give me what I want, and I want you to leave me alone." (Double demand . . . impressive language development!)

And so, for those of us who grew up in comfortable circumstances (yes, I'm talking about you on the laptop), it stands to reason we may need an attitude transplant to progress from "I want to get" to "I want to give." But we can do it! We have the technology to connect with organizations that are doing awesome work. We have credit cards that make spending less painful.

Why wait until December when we're hit up for donations from .orgs we've never heard of and couldn't care less about?

Like E.A.R. (*aka*, Earwax Anxiety Relief). I certainly hope this isn't a real one, but I guess it's too late to check now.

Any time is a good time to look around and see where you could spread a little sunshine and some green. Oxfam America, International Rescue Committee, Good Weave, Doctors Without Borders, UNICEF, and Kiva are some of my personal favorites. And there are at least a million other absolutely inspirational organizations effectively working on solutions to local, national, and international challenges. Giving to any of them makes YOU (and any entitled kid you want to inspire) part of the solution. Find out who's doing what and support their efforts. Start your search with the Charity Navigator.

Warning—Giving can become habit forming, but in a healthy way. Think about it: Do you and your kids really need more stuff or might you be in the market for some good karma points?

REAL WORLD ASSIGNMENT:
Changing the Attitude

Attitudes, like moods, come and go so quickly we often forget that we can decide whether and for how long we want to keep them around. A positive, *giving* attitude can positively infect other people, raising spirits and opening the heart. A negative, self-centered attitude can bring people down and make them feel wary and uncomfortable. We can do much better than that, without pressuring anyone to pretend to be happy all the time.

Listening In—When a teen's need to fit in conflicts with the need to be unique, how can a change in attitude change a young person's life? In this podcast (AnnieFox.com/podcast/FC021.mp3), I talk with award-winning educator, Ronit Baras, author of *Be Special, Be Yourself for Teenagers* (Trafford, 2006).

Fuel for Thought—Hormones, stress, and the self-doubt that fuels it, can throw a relatively easygoing teen into a foul mood. At those times, how can an effective parent-teacher help? Think back to when you were a teen and an adult mentioned your "bad mood" or attitude. What didn't work about that approach? What might have worked better? The golden rule applies to parenting too: If you hated it when you were a kid, don't use it with your kids! Check out these tips for **Improving Parent-Teen Relationships** (QT 7.1).

Conversations That Count—Talk about moods. What's your son or daughter's theory about what causes moods, good or bad? What have they discovered that works to get them out of a bad mood? As long as it's legal and doesn't interfere with the family's core values, it's OK. Share your own "strategies" for getting out of a bad mood. Conversely, what tends to make a bad mood worse?

Teach—Simple relaxation exercises (or getting outside for some fresh air) can help you and your child get back "in balance" when a bad attitude threatens.

WHAT WOULD YOU TEACH HERE?

My mom expects so much from me and always yells at me for the stupidest things. No matter what, she sticks up for my little sister. I try not to yell back but she drives me to that point. I usually just go to my room and cry, but she thinks I'm faking it. All I want is to feel loved the same way she loves my sister. I know she loves me, but sometimes she has a funny way of showing it. With my dad I'm good, because he shows that he loves my sister and me the same. But with my mom it feels like a contest for her love and my sister always gets it. Just because I'm a teen doesn't mean I don't need a hug when she knows I'm feeling bad. It doesn't mean I don't deserve to get more than "Oh, OK. Good," for something I try my hardest on. —13-year-old

Read my reply (AA 7.2)

THE TIMES ARE CHANGING: BEND OR BREAK

No way is it 2012 already! Didn't we just do the Y2K thing? Is it just me, or is one year not actually as long as it used to be? And how about those kids of ours, growing up at warp speed? Probably a good thing we're all too busy to notice them morphing into young adults before our eyes, otherwise how scary would that be? Of course, when it comes to other people's kids we can't miss the changes, but with our own . . . most of us have an acute case of blind spots. Unfortunately, turning a blind eye to reality isn't the most effective way to parent.

Life is all about change. Our #1 challenge is learning how to deal with our feelings, our bodies, our relationships—all constantly changing. (So is every molecule in this desk, but we can save that for another time.) The more I meditate and walk and garden and talk to kids, the more I understand life's changing ways. The more I twist my torso (Hey, it's not painful! It's yoga!), the more I learn how flexibility is the best tool we've got going for us.

"Steady in the winds of change," my yoga teacher reminds us. Steady as she goes. Strong and steady. Those are guiding principles for teaching kids to be good people. But steady doesn't mean stuck, and true strength requires insight into what's needed right now plus the flexibility to adapt.

Suppose you and your teen have always enjoyed a close relationship. S/he always told you about everything that's going on. You've prided yourself on your closeness and how it reflects so positively on your parenting skills. Then one day, around age 12, you walk past your child's room and the door is closed. You walk in. S/he's listening to music and reading. "Hi," s/he says, not removing the earbuds.

You sit on the bed. "How's it going? What's new with you?"

"Nothing."

An awkward silence follows.

"You want something?" your child asks.

You shake your head and slowly walk toward the door. "Uh . . ." your teen begins.

"Yes?" you perk up, expectantly.

"Uh, next time could you please knock instead of just barging in?"

"Sure," you say, feigning a smile as you dislodge the ice pick from your heart. In the hallway your mind reels. *I didn't barge in! And why should I have to knock at my own child's door?! We've never had closed doors between us! Must be hiding something. I'm going back in there and demand to be told what's going on. I was never able to talk to my parents about anything important, but I'm going to make damn sure that me and my child . . .*

WAIT!

What's going on here? Is this about a 12-year-old's normal desire for some privacy and respect or is it about our fear that this relationship is changing into . . . who knows what? In this situation, should we zig or zag? If we zig only because it's how we typically react when we're hurt, then we're not paying attention to our child's needs. Nor are we awake to the current parenting challenge. An unwillingness to change, in spite of changes happening all around, is a surefire formula for ongoing conflicts with our ever-changing kids.

What to do? How about going for a walk? That's usually a mood elevator, but any head-clearing break will help. While we're taking a timeout, it helps to ask: *What does my child need from me now?* It's an essential question whenever we feel confused. A child's assertive behavior expresses a need. Our job? Identify the need as quickly and accurately as possible, then offer help. Of course, nothing we do always works because children's needs change. One moment she'll need a hug and an encouraging word. Another moment he'll need a sympathetic ear and no words at all. Sometimes they'll need clear limits with known consequences for noncompliance. Other times they'll need us to respect their boundaries without taking it personally.

What about *our* changing needs? Where do they come in? That depends. We are absolutely within our rights to have our role, our values, our rules, and our property respected. But we've always got to take care of our own needs. When we use our children to fulfill our emotional needs, including pressuring them to stay home with us when we're lonely or using them to look good in the eyes of others, then we've crossed a line into unhealthy parenting. Our kids have a big enough job learning to take care of themselves without having to take care of us too.

In life, change is our constant companion. Our kids are the clearest evidence of that. As parents, we're privileged to have an essential role in their unfolding. We also have the responsibility of helping them become their best selves. If we pay close attention, we get to witness the process. Another piece of the reward is an opportunity to learn and grow along with them.

It's still very much a new century. Change is the air we breathe. The best we can do for ourselves and our children, is to remain as steady and flexible as possible. It also helps to keep our eyes, mind, and heart open. That's what our kids need most from us.

REAL WORLD ASSIGNMENT:
They're Changing and so Must We

Our children are fast tracking it toward adulthood. Inevitably our role as sole provider of love, sustenance, and guidance must change. The gold ring at the end of the active phase of parenting is a healthy relationship with our independent adult children. To get there, we need to be ever mindful of their changing needs. It's all about gradually stepping back from managing everything for them and encouraging them to step up and manage their own lives.

Fuel for Thought—How did it feel, as a teen, when you were sure your parents underestimated your maturity and good judgment to make your own decisions? How did that struggle play out? At that time, what did you need *more* of from your parents? What did you need *less* of?

Conversations That Count—If your child questions your authority to "tell them what to do," then you've experienced some conflicts. Talk about the typical situations that set off nasty fireworks between you. Ask, "At those times, what do need more of from me? What do you need less of?" Listen to what your son/daughter has to say. Ask your child to pose the same question to you. Frame your answer in the direction of the eight character traits we've been learning about throughout this book.

For example, "I need more respect from you, especially when you're angry and we're having a disagreement. I'm willing to give you more respect too." "I'd like you to be more aware of the way you manage your anger and frustration, and I will do the same."

Tell him or her, "Pushing back against parental authority is normal for teens, everyone does it. I did it too." Also let your child know, "Learning to think for yourself is exactly what you should be doing, but rudeness, disrespect, and irresponsible behavior are unnecessary for you to get the independence you want. This behavior is no longer acceptable in our family. Not from you (your siblings) and certainly not from me." Then please close your mouth and listen to what your child has to say.

———————————

WHAT WOULD YOU TEACH HERE?

My daughter is in sixth grade. She is wearing makeup and dresses provocatively. Most of the other girls in her class do not. One of her friend's parents says my daughter is a bad influence on her daughter! I would prefer she dress more appropriately and not wear makeup. Other moms say that it's not a battle you can win. My husband and my 18-year-old son say I'm overreacting. Am I? —My child's teacher

Read my reply (AA 7.3)

170

MY LIFE SUCKS VS.
THE BIGGER PICTURE

That morning in high school, when they posted the cast list
for *The Music Man*, I pressed forward with the other young
thespians, fully expecting to read my name beside the lead
role of Marion the Librarian.

I didn't get the part. My best friend did.

Stunned, suddenly nauseous, and disconnected from reality,
I attempted to psychically morph the letters of her name into
mine. At that critical moment, my magic powers failed. So
did my ability to see the Bigger Picture (BP).

A parent's life experience enables us to see beyond our
child's botched goal attempt in a tournament and move past
a failed romance. We tend to make our most ethical,
compassionate choices from our BP perspective. That's why
teaching kids about the long view fits so well with teaching
them good character traits. That's our long-term goal. In the
short-term, taking the BP view provides kids with needed
encouragement and solace during tough times.

But before we bore them with mini-lectures about how "this
too shall pass," we should give a kid in the throes of an upset
the chance to vent, grieve, or throw a self-pity party.
Expressing emotion is healthy . . . dumping is not! What's
the difference?

Expressing feelings is about clearing emotional clutter.
Talking helps people understand where we're coming from,
which helps us release pain, which gets us back into the
positive place where we are best able to make good choices

171

that respect our values and benefit others. A toddler screams because, without words, adults often don't "get" what s/he's upset about. Fourteen-year-olds usually scream less because they have language and, if we are patient and provide a safe place to communicate, that leads to more understanding and healthier relationships.

Dumping, on the other hand, is not about communication and understanding. Often, the chief goal is to complain, blame, paint oneself as a victim, and/or avoid responsibility for any part of the "bad stuff" that happened. Dumping rarely leads to healthier relationships.

Here's an example from the dumpster: Your eighth-grade son comes home from a field trip in a foul mood. "Is something wrong?" you ask helpfully. He launches into a rant about: the "jerk" he had to sit next to on the bus, the terrible lunch you made, the tour guide who yelled at him, the fact that his best friend can't take a joke, and how the girl he likes told everyone she thinks he's gay. He finishes with "My life sucks!"

This is dumping, plain and unadulterated. When kids are in the middle of one of these storms, they may sound desperate for help, but they don't really want it. They just want to dump. If you try to help them, they'll turn on you.

Dumping should NEVER be encouraged because it reinforces bad habits, including the eternally off-putting "I'm a victim" attitude. On top of that, dumping doesn't help your child come to terms with what's really going on. So when our children dump, we might respond like this: "Sounds like you've had a really bad day. When you're a little calmer, I'd be happy to help you sort out your feelings so you can resolve some of this. Let me know when you're ready to talk."

We teach compassion by showing them compassion. In this case, it's about truly listening and letting your child know you get it. Be sympathetic. Life's unfair. That is, if "fair" means everyone gets dealt the same hand and is treated in the same way. Nope. Not fair. Acknowledge that. Be sincere. S/he'll calm down, and when s/he does share your understanding of the Bigger Picture. Tell your own version of "I didn't get the lead in *Music Man*"—everyone has one. Make sure you mention what you learned from yours.

For the record, I learned that setbacks are often bundled with opportunities. My best friend was shy and benefited from a chance to be a "star." I had already starred in several plays and definitely didn't need any more ego boosting. What I needed was a chance to support the success of others, which I did as student chorus director. So it all worked out . . . perfectly.

Life is for learning. If we're open and willing to study hard, we take what we learn in this moment and use it to move our kids and ourselves forward. That's the Bigger Picture.

———————————

REAL WORLD ASSIGNMENT:
Seeing the Bigger Picture

Kids can be so caught up in *Me, Myself, and I* that they're blind to anything beyond their immediate feelings. The enormity of those emotions may overwhelm to the point where they believe "I will ALWAYS feel this way!" At emotional times, a parent's teacher-mentor role requires such grace and skill. Teaching our kids to be good people includes helping them learn to be compassionate. We can do that by acknowledging the ragged truth of their raw emotions and by teaching them resilience and courage. How do we perform that complex dance step? By helping our children see that the current emotional storm, while fierce as all get-out, shares a few things with past storms that they've successfully weathered. ("You got through something like this. You can do it again.") In that compassionate reminder, there is much inspiration and encouragement.

Fuel for Thought—Recall a time when you did not survive an emotional upset of your own. I'm not being facetious here. I'm simply stating the obvious (which in times of crisis can be helpful). No matter what has happened to us in the past, no matter how emotionally challenging that event (or period) was, if we are reading these words, then we have survived.

Conversations That Count—Choose a calm time (after an emotional outburst or meltdown) to discuss how difficult it can be to talk rationally when someone is upset. Explain how we all go into Emergency Mode when we're angry, frustrated, jealous, or scared. Recall a recent time when someone in the family was upset and someone else tried to have a reasonable conversation with him/her. What happened?

NOTE: The point of bringing up this past event is *not* to blame the emotional person for having been emotional. The point is to review the incident together and calmly talk about what it was like from each of your perspectives.

Teach—We all get upset at times, feel stuck, and lose the connection with our rational mind. But the most encouraging and special part about being human is our unique ability to talk about feelings. This provides us with enormous opportunity to learn and grown in the direction of Good. The next time your child loses it, let the storm run its course (provided that s/he is not physically or verbally abusing anyone or damaging property). Revisit the plan for Getting Unstuck (QT 3.1) to help your son or daughter get back to seeing the Bigger Picture.

———————————

WHAT WOULD YOU TEACH HERE?

My relationship life sucks! All through middle school I have watched my friends get boyfriends. They've wondered why their friend, who rates a solid 9.5 on looks alone, has an A average, plays basketball and volleyball, and just received my school's top artist award, can't find a guy. Why don't I have any luck in guy-hunting? Am I too tall? Overconfident? I'm not exactly popular, but no one truly holds anything against me.

I realize it's dumb to need to be validated by being in a relationship, but at some point I start wondering what's wrong with me. I feel like I'm

176

doomed to be alone forever!! I want to know what I'm doing wrong so that I don't repeat the mistakes in high school
 —13-year-old

Read my reply (AA 7.4)

8: HOW CAN
I DO THAT?

DEVELOPING
SOCIAL COURAGE

*"Courage is what it takes to stand up and speak;
courage is also what it takes to sit down and listen."*

—Winston Churchill

Courage isn't the absence of fear. Courage is the impulse and conviction to do what's right *in spite of* being afraid. Our children are growing up in a world that is much scarier, faster, louder, and meaner than the one we knew during childhood. They see fewer adults who model social courage. They feel intense pressure to succeed academically and socially. That pressure can cause them to lose sight of what's right. In doing whatever it takes to fit in, many kids make thoughtless choices. And due to the fact that much of their social lives are played out on social media, those choices become part of their indelible digital footprint. When kids who lack social courage repeatedly add to the garbage, their self-perception changes. Instead of thinking of themselves as "good" kids, they may begin to see themselves as people who do unkind things for social gain, without giving it a second thought. Teaching our kids to be good people includes helping them be more courageous and better able to make choices that reflect who they really are.

FRIENDSHIP IS A TWO-WAY STREET

Most parents feel proud to see their kid being a good friend. Friendship skills can tell us whether we're on the right track teaching our children the importance of caring about others. But kids aren't born knowing about respect, cooperation, and empathy. Initially, they learn these lessons from us. One way to teach our kids a whole lot about goodness and friendship is by paying attention to the way we are with them. Showing that we're happy to see them and enjoying their company helps them learn to trust other people. Because of a parent's consistent love and support, little kids often say, "My mom/ dad is my best friend!"

But as kids' friendships with peers get more complex, they need us to help connect the dots and understand that friendship is a two-way street.

If your child is being bullied in a friendship, or is being the aggressor, s/he needs a course correction . . . now! And you're the perfect person to set that change in motion. Tweens make lots of mistakes in friendships, in part because they know how much is riding on peer approval. Their stress (*aka* social anxiety) doesn't improve their decision-making skills. That's why your Bigger Picture perspective can be invaluable. Don't wait until the next friendship betrayal or frenemy crisis. Sit down with your son or daughter ASAP and have a calm, respectful, discussion about friendship. You might say something like this:

Sweetheart, in a real friendship (the only kind worth having) both people need to treat each other with respect. If a friend is only supportive some of the time, the friendship becomes unpredictable . . . and not in a good way. When you can't always count on your friend to be respectful or your friend can't always count on you, the friendship becomes shaky. That's when you need to respect yourself and speak up.

It isn't always easy to tell the truth, even to a best friend. But if you stay silent when you're hurting, things will probably get worse because your friend may believe that you're OK with what's going on. You and I both know you aren't OK with being laughed at or teased or ignored. And since friendship is a two-way street, it works in the other direction too. If you treat a friend in ways you're not proud of, there's a part of you that knows this isn't OK. That's when you've got to be honest.

181

In case you're wondering if speaking up guarantees that you won't ever have any more problems with your friends, the answer is no. If you tell a friend that you've had it with being disrespected, s/he may get angry. This person may accuse you of trying to wreck the friendship. Or, s/he may turn others against you. It's also possible s/he may do all of that and more. Because I'm always honest with you, I'm letting you know there are risks in being true to yourself and honest with other people. But real friends are brave when it comes to doing what's best for a friend. And real friends can take the truth because they know you'd never intentionally hurt them. The truth often strengthens a real friendship, so there's that.

Sweetie, I love you . . . which is why I want you to understand, now while you're in school and for the rest of your life, that you've got to be your own best friend. That means having the courage to let people know where you stand and never giving anyone permission to be mean to you or others.

REAL WORLD ASSIGNMENT:
Real Friends vs. the Other Kind

When friends aren't acting like friends it can be so confusing to kids and adults. The confusion typically coagulates into a question: "What can I do?" Often the answer is not clear to the child because s/he doesn't trust his/her instincts to have "read" the situation accurately. Children may also be unwilling to speak up for fear that they will "make things worse."

Fuel for Thought—Recall your own days in middle and high school and think of the people you considered your real friends. What was it about those relationships that made them so special? When you and your real friends had conflicts, how did you handle them? If you can't recall having any real friends, what's your best theory about why that was the case?

Conversations That Count—Talk with your child honestly about friendship, especially the fact that it is a two-way street. Ask: "How do you know when someone is a real friend? How do you know when you are not being a real friend to someone?" This conversation (and it should be a conversation, not an interview or an interrogation!) can provide great insight into your child's understanding of the nature of friendship. Listen more than you speak. Share some cherished recollections about school friends as well as some disappointments in a friend's behavior and in your own.

Teach—Once you and your child have established standards for being a "real friend" it is easier to have ongoing conversations about friendship issues. Remember: When your child is unhappy in a friendship, it's likely because s/he has a complaint about a friend's behavior. While your child's feelings and perceptions about what's going on are always valid, please help him/her see that a) there are always two sides of the "story" and b) your child always has options for improving the situation. Teach him that complaining to others and not speaking up will probably not make things better in the friendship. Courage propels action and action often results in change. The change that comes may not be what your child imagined or hoped for, but when the status quo is no longer acceptable, something's gotta give.

———————————

WHAT WOULD YOU TEACH HERE?

Two of my best friends always complain about not having a lot of friends, but they are very judgmental about other people. I have a friend that I grew very close to. My two friends call her mean names. They get mad when I hang out with her and other people. I'm kind of stuck because if I mention people they could be friends with they say they don't like them and come up with some excuse as to why. What they don't know is that people are starting not to like them because they are judgmental. —12-year-old

Read my reply (AA 8.1)

BUTT IN LADY.
YOU TOO, MISTER

I don't know how to mind my own business. It's not like I snoop or gossip (much), but when someone looks like they need help I usually offer. When kids are involved, no hesitation.

It's occupational conditioning. Every day teens and tweens invite me into their business through emails like:

☞ "My best gal friend just broke up with her boyfriend and I wanna ask her out, but I don't know how long I should wait."

☞ "Could you tell me anything that would calm down the storm going on in my head?"

☞ "I go to school everyday wanting to cry in the bathroom and stay there forever."

☞ "What can I do to make him understand that I'm not seven years old any more?"

☞ "I'm shy, and that's pretty debilitating in getting friends, standing up to people, or showing my valor. Do you have any techniques to get over that problem?"

They ask: "What should I do?" So I tell them what I think. This has been going on for 15 years, so it's pretty much a habit online and off. But come to think of it, I've been this way for much longer than that. It probably started when I was a fifth grader and joined my school's Safety Patrol. On my first day I was assigned to the kindergarten playground

186

and successfully broke up a shoving match between two very upset five-year olds. Somehow I managed to get them to stop crying and start talking to each other. Afterwards, I watched them go play together, and I've been hooked on helping ever since.

I turned in my silver badge when I moved up to middle school, but my license to butt in never expired. I've stepped right in when I witnessed a kid:

☞ steal an umbrella from a parked car
☞ mercilessly yank her dog's leash
☞ choke his "friend"
☞ mock another kid
☞ tell a racist joke

These kids were messing up and they needed help, so, without being asked, I offered a course-correction. I'm not a hero so don't nominate me. Simple truth, I speak out because I'm afflicted with the "I'm Part of the Village" form of Tourette's, and in these situations I literally cannot keep my mouth shut. (Ask my husband or our children.) I'm sure a muzzle would help, but I'm not looking for a cure. In fact, I'd like to infect all of you.

Kids out in the world on their own make mistakes, and they need corrections from well-intentioned, clear-thinking adults. When they get that timely feedback, especially from a kind stranger, it's a huge wake-up call. Guaranteed, they're less likely to make that mistake again.

So here's what I'm proposing . . . join my Butt In Campaign. It comes with a free license to respectfully speak to any kid who needs to hear that what s/he's doing right now isn't OK. If the idea of spontaneous intervention evokes thoughts of "What other people's kids do isn't my business," I say, I'm not buying it. I mean look where you are. You're reading Annie Fox's book! The only people who show up here take parenting/mentoring very seriously.

Kids growing up right is everyone's business. Which reminds me, your Butt In license also gives you unlimited rights to toss a smile and a passing compliment to any kid who's doing something admirable. "Thanks for holding the door." "Good job helping your dad." "He's lucky to have you as a friend." "What a terrific big sister you are!"

Compliment or course correction, either way, it's not that hard. And even when it is, have courage and think of the good karma points you're racking up.

OK, Butt-inskys. We're in this together, right? Good luck! Let's keep each other posted.

REAL WORLD ASSIGNMENT:
Standing Up for the Underdog

It takes an extra boost of social courage to go out of your comfort zone and show support for someone who is being targeted by others. Maybe we don't do it as often as we should because we're wired to protect our own self-interests. When kids ask me about standing up for someone who is being bullied, I tell them they shouldn't put themselves directly in harm's way, however, there are many ways to show a person, "Others are giving you a hard time. But not me. I'm not like that."

Fuel for Thought—At different points in life we have all been underdog, top dog, and middle of the pack dog, so we know what it feels like to be in each of those places. Being on the bottom and feeling like you've got no support, is probably one of the saddest, loneliest, hopeless times. Think about a time when you helped an underdog. What happened?

Conversations That Count—Talk about the concept of a "pecking order" in the animal kingdom as well as in human society. Make a statement: "Most of the time, when we're not on the bottom, we don't give much thought to those who are." Ask your child what s/he thinks about that. Talk about who is "on the bottom" in your child's class. (Even kids as young as second or third grade have a keen awareness of social strata.) How do other people treat that child? How do you treat him/her? What might happen if you stood up for the under dog?

Teach—Challenge your child to be a hero and shake up the social strata by standing up for someone who needs a friend. Follow up and find out from your child what happened.

———————————

WHAT WOULD YOU TEACH HERE?

I have a friend that's a victim of bullying every day in school. He only confessed that to me. I said that he could talk with a teacher to ask for help, but he doesn't want that because he's afraid that the aggressors will hit him again. He doesn't want my help for the same reason. I don't know what to do or who to tell. Help me please.
—12-year-old

Read my reply (AA 8.2)

PEER APPROVAL ADDICTION GROUP MEETS HERE

I jumped right in. If I couldn't let these seventh-grade girls know a) I get middle school friendship issues, b) they could trust me to listen with compassion and respect, and c) this was a safe place to talk about stuff that really mattered, it was going to be a long and pointless hour.

My PowerPoint began with the slide of a sad-faced girl beside this email:

> *Hey Terra,*
>
> *When me and my friend are alone we have a lot of fun. But when she's with her other friends, she doesn't talk to me at all. What do I do?*
>
> *—Invisible Friend*

"Who can relate to this situation?" I asked the group, raising my own hand high.

The girls shot each other furtive glances, but otherwise didn't move. I advanced to the next slide.

> *Hey Terra,*
>
> *My friends don't want to be my friend any more. They pick on me. They whisper and then look at me and laugh. When I try to make new friends they seem to steal them away from me by telling lies. My mom wants to talk to the other*

parents, but I don't want her to because it will make it worse! How do I deal with them?

—*Lonely*

"Does this one ring any bells for you?" I asked the girls. "It sure does for me." My hand felt lonely hovering in the air above my head.

Again I advanced:

Hey Terra,

When I'm with these three boys at school we get in trouble. I know they're not the nicest guys, but I don't really have any other friends at the moment. Also, I'm afraid if I don't hang out with them and do what they do, they might do something to me!

—*Lost*

"How about this one, girls? C'mon. Be honest. Who's been there?"

For the third time the girls scoped each other out, their groupthink warned everyone to keep a low profile. Yet, this time, when my hand went up one girl joined me! Before I could acknowledge her courage, she retreated. Probably hoping against hope that she hadn't just ruined her entire life.

"Have any of you ever heard of Peer Approval Addiction?" I asked. "No worries. It's something I made up. Let me explain it. You know the word addiction, as in drug addiction?"

They all nodded. True, this showed they were listening, and I might have taken some encouragement from it, but I'm well aware that a key element of Good Girl Code requires that you impress adults with your maturity and intelligence whenever possible. Just because they were willing to nod "Yes, we know the word addiction" didn't necessarily mean they were brave enough to talk about the friendship issues we were there to discuss.

"Addiction is an out-of-control behavior. Addicts continue the behavior despite negative consequences to their mental or physical health, or to their relationships. In other words, when they do this thing, it makes big problems for them. But they keep doing it anyway because they feel like they have no other choice. Just like the boy in the last email. Peer Approval Addiction is doing whatever it takes to fit in and be accepted by the people around you. That could mean doing stuff you're not proud of or holding yourself back from doing what you want to do. That's what's going on right here. That's why you're not raising your hands, even though you've had problems with friendships and you'd really like to talk about it.

"I just want to let you know that you don't have to keep pretending. I know there have been times when you've felt just like "Invisible Friend" and like "Lonely" and "Confused." We all have. At least once in your life, you've probably felt like you wanted to get out of a friendship because you weren't comfortable with the way your friend was acting. At least once or maybe twice, you've been hurt when a friend turned against you and you didn't have a clue why or what to do about it.

"Look, I know it can be scary to publicly admit that you've been dissed, ditched, or dumped by a so-called friend. I know

193

you're thinking, "If I raise my hand here and no one else does, someone's going to tease me."

"You're not the only one who feels this way. All of us, teens and adults, have held ourselves back from telling the truth or doing the right thing because we were worried what others would think. So all of us are a little peer approval addicted. I know I sure am. How about you?"

I raised my hand and so did every single girl in the room.

We were making progress and we still had a full 54 minutes to go.

REAL WORLD ASSIGNMENT:
Social Courage

They say that *character* is demonstrated by the choices we make when we believe that no one is watching. *Social courage* is doing the right thing in broad daylight, when everyone is watching. Of the two, the latter is much more challenging, especially for peer-conscious tweens and teens.

Listening In—T(w)een friendships can be fraught with emotional drama, which proves that being emotional doesn't automatically translate into high Emotional Intelligence. In this podcast (AnnieFox.com/podcast/FC011.mp3), I talk with Rachel Simmons, founder of Girls Leadership Institute, and author of the *New York Times* best-selling *The Curse of the Good Girl: Raising Authentic Girls with Courage and Confidence* (Penguin Group, 2010).

Fuel for Thought—What is a peaceful warrior? How do we show our adult peers that we stand for fairness, for kindness, for peace? How do we show our children that this is who we are and who we expect them to be?

Conversations That Count—Share this quote with your son/daughter: "The time is always right to do what is right." — Martin Luther King, Jr.

Ask, "What do you think of this? True? Too simplistic?" Talk about a time when you or someone else was being treated unfairly and you stepped up and did the right thing. What happened? If you or your child can't recall a time like that, perhaps you can talk together about a time when you didn't do what is right to help promote peace and fairness. What held you back?

Teach—Random Acts of Courage. We can all agree that people should treat one another with respect at all times. In order to make progress in that direction, each of us needs to become more courageous. Create a family challenge to increase your acts of social courage over the next couple of weeks. You'll need some paper strips (11 x 2 inches), some tape, and a pen. (Or you can just make a list.)

☞ Start with what you just shared about a time you stepped up and did the right thing when someone needed a friend or a message of peace.

☞ Write a sentence about what you did on one strip of paper. Sign your name.

☞ Connect your strip with someone else's and create "links" using tape.

☞ Got more than one act of social courage? Make another link!

☞ Each day keep adding to the chain by actively looking for opportunities to be "brave" in situations where a peaceful warrior is need.

———————————

196

WHAT WOULD YOU TEACH HERE?

According to my friend, my 13-year-old daughter has been mean to her daughter by excluding her and talking behind her back. My first priority is teaching my daughter how to treat other people well, even those we don't want to be friends with. She is going through a rough time due to my divorce, and she's angry at her father because he lied and cheated. I know that divorce is not an excuse for my daughter's mean behavior, but it may be a cause.

—My child's teacher

Read my reply (AA 8.3)

197

AT HOME
IN THE WORLD

The customs official in Houston handed back our passports and said, "Welcome, home." My eyes instantly welled up. Admittedly I'm an emotional marshmallow. I worry about one-legged pigeons in the park. I rush to the aid of droopy plants in restaurants. But to cry at such an innocuous greeting, well that's just ridiculous, isn't it? I wasn't so sure. Maybe my reaction had something to do with the trip we'd just completed.

Now if you're picturing some foreign vacation from hell, you'll need to switch channels. Instead imagine white sand beaches on the Caribbean, jungles, monkeys, sloths, rainforests, an active volcano, and the people we love most in the world sharing it with us. David and I had been to Costa Rica visiting our college-age son and his girlfriend who were studying there. Our daughter joined us from London.

After a sweet reunion packed with lots of laughs and some amazing adventures, it was sad to say goodbye to the kids. I know they're not kids any more, but still . . . The only thing that eased the pain was realizing how fully capable they are of being on their own. They demonstrated that exceptionally well by taking over most of the details of the trip. Working as a team, the "kids" planned our itinerary, made our reservations, and served as guides and translators. We loved the role reversal and greatly appreciated all their efforts on our behalf. They acted like the thoughtful, caring, capable adults they are.

Ultimately, that's what all parents want their kids to become —fully functioning, thoughtful, compassionate adults who are unafraid of life. But we're genetically predisposed to protect them and sometimes we unwittingly hold them back. So how do we quell our own fears and help our children do what they're genetically predisposed to do, i.e., leave the shelter of our family and make their own way? How do we nurture without smothering? Encourage without overreaching? What parenting choices support the resourcefulness our kids need to blossom and feel at home with themselves, no matter where they are?

Big questions. No easy answers.

When I was 15 my father died suddenly. Even though I continued living at the same address until I left for college, it never again felt like home to me. That's probably when I began looking for something that couldn't be lost or taken away—a feeling of home inside of myself.

When we meet someone who is truly at home in the world we are drawn to him/her. It's as if that person puts others at ease by osmosis, but there's nothing mystical about it. Their own self-acceptance has expanded to include other people. When you're on the receiving end of that kind of acceptance, you can relax and enjoy what you're doing and whom you're with on a whole new level. Being at home with yourself is a life skill worth acquiring for your own benefit and for the benefit of others.

It's June and many parents are celebrating their kids' graduation from elementary school. From middle school. From high school. From college. Major transitions. Big changes in store for your kids and for the whole family. How confident are they in their ability to cope with and adapt to what's ahead? How fearless? Hopefully you are right on track for teaching them the important things they need to know about being good and doing good in the world. Hopefully, they will honor you with the choices they make.

So kiss them goodbye, then watch them take off. And like the customs guy, always be there to welcome them home.

REAL WORLD ASSIGNMENT:
Citizens of the World

Most children's lives are confined to their community (neighborhood, school). Yet the world they are becoming a part of is one in which faraway lands and ideas of people with different experiences are more easily accessible than ever. Teaching 21st century kids to be good people includes helping them be accepting of and comfortable with all kinds of people. With this self-confidence, they will be brave enough to do good things, near and far.

Fuel for Thought—When you were growing up in what ways did you think about the wider world and your place in it? How (if at all) has your attitude about meeting new people and experiencing new places changed now that you're an adult? Refer to this plan: How to Raise Young Adults Who Are at Home with Themselves (QT 8.1).

Conversations That Count—Talk to your child about the feeling of being "at home" vs. "not feeling at home." Find out what your child thinks about these two experiences. Ask, "Where have you felt 'at home' when you weren't actually in your own home? What made that place, those people, so welcoming? What role might attitude (being open to new experiences vs. closed) have in helping us feel 'at home' wherever we are?"

Teach—Agree that no one likes feeling like an "outsider." Make a family agreement to work toward being more welcoming to people who are new to the community. If your family is new to the community, challenge yourselves for the next week (at work, at school, on weekends) to learn new things about where you live, including the other people who live there. Reach out to new people. Meet up again and talk about your progress in making yourselves "at home."

WHAT WOULD YOU TEACH HERE?

I just recently moved to a new school from one I'd been in since kindergarten. I am now in seventh-grade. I made what I thought were best friends there, but now a new girl at my old school is "taking my place." I'm really upset about it, and I think my friends don't realize what's going on.

—12-year-old

Read my reply (AA 8.4)

A FINAL WORD

Throughout this monumental, exhausting, and exhilarating parenting journey we step back a little each year so our children can step up to manage more of their own lives, just as they are meant to. Our imperative, as mothers and fathers, is to work our way out of a job so they will need us less and less. But if we parent well, what we've taught our kids will continue to guide them . . . for good.

AA: ANNIE'S ANSWERS TO "WHAT WOULD YOU TEACH HERE?"

CHAPTER 1

AA 1.1 *"My stepson rules the family."* It can be tricky to create a harmonious three-way dynamic between child, parent, and stepparent. Raising a child with special needs presents additional challenges. This situation is not going to resolve itself. Continuing as you have is only likely to create more tension in the marriage and the family. Talk with your wife, calmly and respectfully. Tell her how you've been feeling and listen to what she has to say. Get outside help to provide more effective parenting strategies. Take what you've learned from a professional and work together with patience and a healthy sense of humor to teach your son how to manage his emotions in more responsible ways. Do that and you and your wife will be creating a more peaceful family life and a wonderful legacy for your boy.

AA 1.2 *"I'm worried my friend will smoke pot!"* I admire you for being such a caring person. Whether your friend knows it or not, she's lucky to have you as a friend. What she says about "everyone" trying pot in high school just isn't true. It's also a weak excuse for doing something so dangerous. As her friend, educate yourself about the risks of drug use, what marijuana does to the body and brain, I and where smoking pot can lead. Then you can educate her. The facts might help wake her up, but don't get your hopes up too high. If she has crushes on guys who smoke, part of her probably thinks that smoking pot is "cool." As long as she believes that, she's probably not going to value what you say. But try and talk with her anyway. Real friends don't stay silent when they're worried about a friend.

Ultimately, though, she's going to do whatever she wants. That's the way it is in life. We only have control over our own behavior, not anyone else's. That said, if you have real evidence that she's using drugs, tell her what you know. Tell her that you love her and that what she's doing is harmful to her health. Tell her that if she doesn't stop, you're going to have to talk to her parents and let them know so they can get involved. She's not going to like that, but if she needs help, getting it for her is the most important thing.

AA 1.3 *"Is it a good idea to 'surprise kiss' this guy?"* I understand how exciting it is to imagine hugging and kissing your crush, like in an amazingly romantic movie. But in real life, what you're thinking of doing is not a good idea. You and your friend are making plans about a human being. This boy has feelings and you're acting like only your feelings count. You're also assuming that he wants to be kissed by you at that moment in front of other people. Big assumption!

How would you feel if some guy grabbed you and hugged you and kissed you on the lips when you didn't want that? I'm guessing you wouldn't appreciate it at all. I suggest you rethink your plan.

AA 1.4 *"How do I deal with my bf's rudeness?"* It sounds like you and your bf have communication challenges. Whenever someone you're in a relationship with (parent, sibling, friend, bf/gf) does something that "really annoys" you, you have to speak up. I know it can be awkward, especially if the other person has a short fuse, but how else do you expect him to understand how you feel? No one can read minds!

The next time you're with your bf, just the two of you, and things are calm, you might start a conversation with something like this: "I want us to be able to talk with each other honestly. It really bothers me when you get mad and say embarrassing things to me or just walk away. Especially when we're around other people. I want to talk about this." See what happens. If you two can't communicate respectfully, then this relationship will continue having problems.

CHAPTER 2

AA 2.1 *"How do I stop liking someone who is mean to me?"* You say, "If I made a problem out of [his meanness to me] I could risk losing him." I can understand your being worried about losing a positive relationship with someone who cares about you. But based on the way you describe this guy's behavior ("he is a horrible person to me") what exactly are you worried about "losing"?

By his consistent rudeness he has made it very clear that he does not value you as a person. I understand that you like him, but honestly, do you like the rudeness? Do you like being brushed aside as if your feelings don't count? When he is mean to you he is adding to the social garbage at your school. When you "pretend these things don't hurt" you are also adding to the garbage.

Please stop demeaning yourself. You deserve much better than the treatment you're getting. The sooner you refuse to settle for disrespect from this guy or anyone, the sooner you will find the kind of relationships you are looking for.

AA 2.2 *"How do I keep my daughter from making more bad choices?"* You need to get to the bottom of what's going on here, quickly. Yes, you could blame it on friends of whom you "disapprove." But that's not helpful, and dissing her friends is just going to alienate your daughter. While peers have influence, ultimately the choices your daughter is making are her own. She's a smart girl who's decided that crossing the line isn't that big a deal. Because you don't want this pattern of poor judgment to continue, I strongly suggest you find a psychologist or licensed marriage and family therapist who specializes in working with teens. Get a few recommendations, and allow your daughter to "interview" the candidates. It's important she find a professional whom she trusts. That way she will have a safe place to talk about some of the things that are motivating her to step out of her "honor roll student" box. In the safe place, she's more likely to hear your concern and your respectful guidance.

AA 2.3 *"How does a single mom talk to her son about respecting girls?"* You might say something like this, "You are old enough to have girlfriends. And I know that there are girls you like. That's why I want to talk to you about boyfriend/ girlfriend relationships. You may think it's all about what you want. But a relationship is a two-way street. If you want a good girlfriend, you have to be a good boyfriend. Tell me what you think it means to be a good boyfriend."

Then close your mouth, and listen to what he has to say. I'm guessing he's never thought about it in this way before. He may just shrug and say, "I don't know."

That's when you say, "OK. I understand that you may not know. After all, they don't teach classes in this in school, though they probably should. But guys need to learn it, so I'm going to teach you. I can tell you what being a good boyfriend means from the girl's point of view. Here's what you need to know: No girl likes to be pressured into doing things she's not ready for. Guys who pressure girls to 'do stuff' are being disrespectful. The kind of girls who make the best girlfriends are girls with self-respect. They will stand up for themselves. They will say, 'No, I'm not going to do that. And I don't like it when you pressure me. So just stop.'"

Say: "You know you've got the right to tell someone to stop pressuring you, so what do you think about a girl's right to tell you to stop?"

Listen for his answer. Ultimately you want him to realize that as his mom, it's your responsibility to teach him to treat people with respect. That includes teachers, friends, kids he may not particularly like, and girlfriends. This isn't about sex, it's about respect and empathy (taking the other person's point of view).

Tell your son you have some information that he's been pressuring girls to do things they don't want to do. Tell him this is wrong. Finish it up like this: "Maybe you didn't know it was wrong before we had this conversation, but now you do. From now on, I expect you to always treat people with respect. If I find out that isn't the case, there will be a consequence. We understand each other, right?" Right.

AA 2.4 *"What if I want my daughter to go along with the crowd?"* I'm not sure what you think your daughter needs to "learn the hard way" or any way for that matter. And while we're clearing stuff up, how can anyone possibly go "overboard" in being themselves? That's like saying, "You are too much of who you are."

You say, "I want her to be herself" . . . but do you really? What I'm hearing loud and clear sounds like "The way she is, is unacceptable! I want her to be more like everyone else." If that's where you're coming from, your daughter feels the sting of your disapproval every day. That's not helpful.

The only positive thing you said about your daughter is that she's "not boy crazy." Surely she possesses many admirable traits, but you didn't mention any. That's a sign this girl isn't getting much positive feedback from her mom. You are her most influential teacher. Giving her positive reinforcement will go a long way in helping her build self-esteem.

It sounds like you believe your daughter has a problem and if she'd only "listen" to you all would be well. I disagree. I'm sure your advice is well-meaning and that you are a loving parent. But your daughter is a strong individual, and while her fashion sense might make you uncomfortable at times, she should be acknowledged for having the courage of her convictions. Props to her for all that self-confidence!

There could be a number of reasons contributing to her rejecting girly clothes, but instead of taking the point of view that she is purposely defying anyone, it might help if you saw all of this as her journey of self-discovery.

I don't mean to give you a hard time. All of us dream of what our child will grow up to be. Maybe your daughter's current behavior, choice of clothing, etc., is a disappointment to you. Maybe her way of being is embarrassing to you as you watch the reactions she gets from peers and other adults. Please be honest with yourself about your feelings, but don't share them with your daughter. She doesn't need to hear it.

Bottom line, your daughter is who she is and trying to get your approval by pretending to be someone other than her authentic self is not healthy. That would only encourage her to live a lie and put her in conflict with herself. Not the advice she needs.

Obviously, your child isn't you. And it's not her job to fulfill your expectations of who you think she is "supposed" to be. She is her own wonderfully unique self. She doesn't need fixing. She needs the unconditional love of her mom. In order to support her journey into adulthood, wherever it may lead, please stop trying to change her, and start trying to understand her better.

CHAPTER 3

AA 3.1 *"Why don't my parents give me more money?"* It sounds like you are blaming your parents (just a little) for the fact that you were "desperate" enough to steal. Nothing your parents did caused you to steal. You knew it was wrong, and there was a chance you would get caught. And you chose to do it anyway. So please take responsibility for what you did. That is the only way that you can avoid making those kinds of choices.

OK, now . . . moving forward. Your mother is upset and disappointed. She may be angry and hurt as well. You want more independence, and to get that you need to rebuild the trust that you've damaged. It's going to take time and a "new history" to show your parents that you know how to make good choices. The first step would be to apologize to them for the hurt you caused. That might help heal things between you. You also should be thinking about what you learned through all of this. Hopefully you've learned something about choices and consequences, so the next time you feel "desperate" to get some money for going out with girls, etc., you will find ways to earn it and not ever steal again. When you figure out what you've learned, talk to your parents. Explain your new way of thinking to them. Consistently make healthier choices, and over time, you will help heal the relationship.

AA 3.2 *"How can I do all my chores and homework faster?"*
These are some pretty tough times you're going through. And you are doing an *amazing* job helping your family! I'm sure your parents are very proud of you and so appreciative of all your help. If your teachers aren't aware of what's going on at home, tell them. That will help them understand that they ought to ease up on you at this time. Talking to a school counselor might also help get the message to the teachers and give you some emotional support for what you're going through.

As for a "system" to get stuff done faster: Make a list of your responsibilities at home, what you need to do every day vs. a few times a week. That might help you feel more organized and in control of what could easily feel like a mountain of work. Would your life be easier if you didn't have homework and cooking and cleaning to do? Absolutely! But things are the way they are . . . for now. They won't always be this way. In the meantime, here's the best advice I can give: Do what you need to do to fulfill your responsibilities to your family and your schoolwork. Then make sure you schedule time every single day *for yourself*, even if it's only 30 or 60 minutes. Time to chill is one way to help yourself. You totally deserve it.

AA 3.3 *"I tell people I'm fine but I think I have an eating disorder."* Everything is obviously *not* "fine." Your mom is worried about you. People at school who offer you their food are worried about you. The Dean of Students is worried about you. And since you just wrote to me for help, I'd say it's safe to deduce that *you* are worried about you!

Anyone can develop an eating disorder, and it definitely sounds like you are severely restricting calories (possibly to avoid being teased). Now it sounds like you have gotten into a habit of not eating. I'm guessing that when you do eat you're not enjoying the food at all. (An energy bar is not a complete, ongoing source of the nutrients your body needs.)

I'm going to add myself to the list of people who care about you and are worried about you. You say, "I don't know what to do any more." Here's what you need to do today: Talk to your mom. Tell her the *truth*. Tell her what you told me . . . about not eating . . . about feeling depressed. Tell your mom that you don't want to feel this way any more, and you want help. Tell her that you want to talk with the Dean of Students and/or a school counselor.

AA 3.4 *"My son has anger management problems."* This is a dangerous situation because your son's behavior is out of control. He's angry about many things, and he doesn't know how to express his emotions in ways that don't endanger himself and others. This must be addressed immediately.

213

It's a good sign that he apologized after his latest outburst. That shows he knows what he did was wrong. If he has a good relationship with the youth minister, then that person would be an excellent resource for you. Find out if the youth minister has any kind of counseling background. If not, then it's fine to start with the youth minister, but you should also get a referral to a licensed family therapist.

Talk to your son, assuming that he is now calm enough to listen. Tell him that you love him and that you know he is a good person. Tell him also that you know he isn't proud of the way he sometimes loses control. Tell him that you are still very upset about what happened and that you understand that his intense feelings have gotten out of control. Tell him that you are on his side and that you want to help him grow up to be a good man who has the inner strength and self-control to always treats people with respect—even when he is angry.

Tell him that you'd like him to talk with the youth minister, for starters, and see if the two of them can work to together on some anger management skills. Hopefully he will comply and recognize that he needs help. Unless the youth minister is also a psychologist or a licensed therapist, I strongly suggest that you also get a professional evaluation. Your son is the "squeaky wheel" but he is not "the one and only problem" here. This is a family problem, and because that's the case, the boy's father as well as your husband should be involved. I hope you all come together in a professionally supported process that addresses your son's needs and the well-being of the whole family.

CHAPTER 4

AA 4.1 *"My best friend is mean to me."* Let's be honest, he's not your "best friend in the entire world." Maybe it was true in the past, but it isn't true at the moment. You know that best friends do not treat each other the way he is treating you! Have you talked to him privately about this? If not, you should. But even if you have an honest conversation, there are no guarantees that he will suddenly wake up, apologize, and become a real friend again. Those days are gone for now. For now, you need to say to yourself "I deserve to be treated with respect. My friend isn't treating me like a real friend. I am not going to allow him (or anyone) to make me feel small and 'less than.' I'm going to stop feeling sorry for myself. I'm going to leave him alone. He has the right to make a new friend, and so do I."

AA 4.2 *"We found drugs in our kids' rooms!"* You must have suspected something otherwise you wouldn't have searched the rooms. Now with your suspicious confirmed, you need to tell your kids what you know. Your #1 job is to keep them safe. (Teaching them to be good people is job #2.) Do not apologize when they get all huffy and self-righteous because you snooped through their stuff.

Misusing and/or abusing over-the-counter (OTC) drugs are dangerous behaviors and very common with teens. According to a recent survey from Partnership for a Drug-Free America, "40 percent of teens believe that OTC drugs are much safer than illegal drugs." Even if what you found is Niacin (vitamin B3), your son has it because some pot smokers believe it can help them pass drug tests. That's not necessarily true, and Niacin, taken in large dosages can cause toxic reactions!

215

Your kids' thinking about these substances is wrongheaded. You need to educate them. You also need to find out which of their friends might be participating/supplying so you can let their parents know ASAP. Your kids won't be thrilled with your calling other parents. Don't worry about that. If other moms and dads knew about your child's involvement in something like this, you'd fully expect them to inform you, right? You'd be justifiably angry if they didn't, correct? So, it's a no-brainer for a responsible parent. Do the right thing.

Teens and drugs are a huge problem. You need to help your kids understand why drug use is dangerous and totally UNACCEPTABLE in your family. Start a series of conversations with your children. Talk about the need for safety. Search the Internet together to find scientific information about the physical and psychological risks of using these substances. Talk about trust and betrayal, and listen to what they have to say. Discuss appropriate discipline and follow through with your agreements. If your kids are resistant to participating fully in this discussion, you're going to need professional parenting support.

As for searching their rooms, teens deserve our trust unless they betray it. By using drugs your son and daughter have lost your trust and some of their independence—both of which they'll have to earn back. But do not say something like: "You'll be un-grounded when I feel I can trust you again." That's too open ended! Too non-specific! Instead, provide clear expectations for their behavior. ("Here's the behavior I need to see to begin trusting you again.") Also give them a specific timeframe for being on "probation," and closely monitor their progress.

From a parenting perspective, this is about safety even more than it is about trust. Your job is to keep your kids safe and

216

healthy so they can grow up to be good people. Sometimes that includes keeping them safe from themselves.

AA 4.3 *"Sometimes I've got a sarcastic sense of humor, but what he did was worse!"* It sounds like two mistakes were made here. One involves the unkind remarks you've made to team members. Not good. You think you are "just kidding" when you're being funny, but I'd suggest you take this feedback to heart. Apologize to anyone you've hurt with your sarcasm. That will make people feel better, which will make you feel better too. Forgive yourself for your mistakes, and in the future, watch your mouth. I used to be very sarcastic with my humor. Something I learned may help you: Just because a smart remark pops into your head, doesn't mean you have to say it!

By the way, you write very well. Perhaps you write short stories? If so, put those funny lines into the mouths of your characters. That way, you can redirect your humor so no one gets hurt.

As for mistake #2, the guy made that one when he called you out in front of the team with the intention to hurt and embarrass you. That was just plain wrong. I don't think you owe him an apology, but you two should have a private conversation. Tell him that you did not appreciate the way he spoke to you. From now on, if he has an issue with you, he should talk to you in private. That's respectful. You might also tell him that you've been thinking about what he said. Tell him that you now realize you haven't always been sensitive to people's feelings. Tell him you're working on it. Then do just that.

AA 4.4 *"Does my mom have the right to embarrass me in public?"* Sounds like you and your brother lost it at the

217

restaurant. I understand that your brother "started it," but you've got to learn how to stay in control and not let him push your buttons. As for the driving thing, your mom's got a point. There's a strong connection between maturity and safe driving skills. As a driver, you've got to *stay in control* of your emotions as well as your car—otherwise people can get seriously hurt.

You were embarrassed by what your mom said. She was also embarrassed by the way her teenage sons behaved. She said some things she shouldn't have (especially not in public). To answer your question, no, you can't turn your mother in for saying you were "immature," etc. Here's my advice. Cool off. Let her cool off. For the rest of the day, be cool with your brother. If he tries to "start" another fight, show that you have the maturity to stay cool.

Tomorrow, or the day after, have a serious talk with your mom. First, apologize for your behavior. Take responsibility for what you did. Do *not* say, "He started it!" Offer to pay back the $45. (Figure out a way to make it up to her . . . that shows maturity.) Then talk to her, respectfully, about wanting to take driver's ed. Stay calm and see if you and your mom can work out a deal.

CHAPTER 5

AA 5.1 *"I feel forced to be mean just to fit in!"* I can tell you are a good-hearted person because you are bothered by the way your friends are acting. You don't feel right when you act in the same cruel way they do. Your self-awareness is your friend. It's your Inner Voice, and if you listen to it, it can guide you in the direction of being a good person who is kind and caring.

I understand that it can be scary to leave one group and go to another. Especially if you're worried that your old friends may turn some of their meanness on you. I'll be honest, that might happen. And it might not. But what are your choices? If you stay with these girls and continue to do things that hurt other people you will be adding to the bullying and meanness in your school. I'm sure your school already has plenty of that so why add more? Also, if you stick with them you will lose respect for yourself. On the other hand, if you leave to be with "nicer" girls, you will be adding to what is good about your school. You could feel more "at home" and happier. You're also likely to feel proud of yourself. The choice is yours. Good luck!

AA 5.2 "Why won't my mom let me do anything?" You assume your mom trying to control you and you resent it. You don't understand her point of view, and you're frustrated because she isn't explaining herself. You're probably also annoyed that she doesn't seem to understand how important independence is to you. I don't know what your mom's "problem" is, but it could be that she has big worries about your safety when you're not home.

Here's my suggestion: Tell your mom that you would like to talk with her about something important. Pick a time when she is not stressed, rushing out the door, etc. Focus on your feelings, and talk with her calmly and respectfully. (Parents appreciate that.) You might say something like this: "Mom, I don't like it when we fight. I want us to communicate better. I want to understand your feelings, and I want you to understand mine. When you tell me I can't do something without giving me a real reason, I feel _____ (frustrated, angry, annoyed, irritated, sad, hopeless, etc.—fill in the blank with what's true for you). I know you love me and want me to be safe. I want to prove to you that I know how to be careful so that you won't worry so much. Could we please

219

work together on a plan so I can get a bit more independence and you feel more relaxed when I'm with my friends?"

Try that and see what she says. If she feels that you are making a sincere effort to understand her perspective, she may try to do the same with you.

AA 5.3 *"Did we overreact when we grounded her?"* Hard to say if you "overreacted" since I didn't hear the volume level of your discussions with your daughter or the tone of voice and language you used. But one thing is clear: your daughter is too young to be going out with an 18-year-old guy. You made that clear to her. Then she defied you and chose to sneak around and lie, etc. Taking away the tech toys and grounding her seems appropriate. Whether your discipline is effective, time will tell.

You ask: "How do I get my daughter to understand our perspective and respect our decision so she doesn't continue this behavior?"

It's very difficult to get a 15-year-old to "understand" anyone's perspective that differs with her own. Does that mean that you are powerless and must stand by and allow her to continue defying your rules and possibly engaging in high-risk behavior? Absolutely not! You are her parents. If she doesn't change her attitude through loss of privileges, then I'd suggest you go, as a family, to meet with a family therapist. In a neutral setting with a trained professional, it is likely that communication will improve.

Round two from Dad—*I have set up a family therapist meeting. I'm worried because when I told my daughter she freaked out stating, "Oh nice, now you think I am all screwed up and need counseling!" I certainly hope all this pays off and she gets past this.*

I fear a Romeo and Juliet thing happening here: the more I say no to this forbidden love, the more they will pursue.

My reply—You're doing the right thing on all fronts. Clearly express your expectations for her behavior. Catch her in the act of doing something right, and praise her for every step toward maturity and responsible action. And when she slips up (which will happen from time to time) be consistent with your discipline. Don't engage with her "freaked out" behavior. Simply state the facts: "We love you and we need help, as a family, to learn to communicate better. This isn't just about you, sweetheart, this is about all of us . . . together."

Good luck with the therapist, but don't expect miracles after one session. If you all like the therapist, stay committed to the process. If this one isn't a good match, then look for another. Stick with it. The teen years are challenging for kids and parents. It gets easier for them and for us. But during this phase, it's important for parents to lead the efforts of the family working together to build healthier relationships.

AA 5.4 "My mom doesn't understand I'm still me even if I like to dress this way." I'm impressed with your understanding of what might be causing your mom's freak out when she sees you dressed in black. She's pasting onto you, all her negative biases about people who dress like that. She's reacting emotionally rather than thinking things through. Because she has these biases, and she loves you very much, she's feeling scared and threatened and worried.

The best way to convince your mom you are the same loving young man who cares about others and makes ethical choices is to continue doing just that. If you do, my guess is, that she will begin to relax and realize that the clothes have not changed you in an unhealthy way.

221

One more suggestion: There may be times (like family events, for example) where she'll be super aware of what other people think. At those times, if you'd be willing to tone down "the look" Mom would probably appreciate that. It's a funny thing about perception. Parents are often hypersensitive about how other people view their kids and she wouldn't want anyone (especially family members) to think you've turned into "the devil."

So, talk to her. Ask her to give you a chance to show what an excellent parenting job she's done and that you are still a great guy that she can be proud of.

CHAPTER 6

AA 6.1 *"Even if it's stupid, it hurts to see my little sister suffering."* It is NOT "stupid" to feel the pain and suffering of others. It's is a sign of compassion. You are a kind-hearted person. Your sister is very lucky to have you in her life. You say, "I can't stand watching!" then DO something to help your sister. Talk with your parents (calmly and respectfully) about what you have observed. Step in and help your sister when she seems "sad," especially when she is lonely or when your parents are "rude" to her. With your support she will feel that she is not alone. Her big brother is her friend and watches over her. That can mean so much! Being a hero to your sister will also help you see what a strong and loving young man you are and why you should never let anyone bring you down.

AA 6.2 *"Our daughter is respectful to everyone but her parents."* You're on to something when you say, "It's almost as if she cannot control herself." She can't! At least, not very easily. At 14, her psychological imperative is to fight her way to her own identity. To do that she may temporarily need to create distance by disagreeing with you at every turn and intersection. When you ask for her cooperation, she balks because part of her believes that doing what Mom and Dad say is acting "like a child," and she's way more mature and independent than that! How ironic. But from a parent's perspective, a teen's rudeness is a clear indication of how immature s/he still is.

As frustrating and hurtful as this is, I believe it is a phase and will pass. When your 14-year-old acts out, you can help the situation by staying calm. (Not easy, but you have to try.) Does staying calm mean you should allow your daughter to show disrespect? Definitely NOT!

That's why you should sit down with her today and establish family ground rules moving forward. Tell her that you have dropped the ball recently by letting her speak to you disrespectfully without any real consequences. Apologize for this lapse in good parenting. Tell her you now realize that by letting her get away with rudeness you've taught her it's OK to be disrespectful, which it is not. You've also missed many opportunities to let her know that self-respecting adults don't accept disrespectful treatment from anyone (including their own children). For all of this, you apologize and pledge to do a better job as her parent.

Explain to your daughter what kind of behavior you expect from her from now on. Let her know that while you appreciate that it's hard sometimes to stay in control of what we say when we're upset, you have full confidence that she can learn to do it. Also let her know that her cooperation will be appreciated and acknowledged. If she doesn't comply with the rules, she gets a consequence for her behavior. (Be it taking away her phone for a day, or taking away her computer, or grounding her from activities. Consequences work when you find what matters to your daughter.)

After you and your husband put the new policy in place, the rest is straightforward. As soon as you detect any attitude from your daughter, simply say in a neutral voice, "That tone of voice is not acceptable. If you continue talking to me that way, there will be a consequence." Plain and simple. No yelling. No threatening. No disrespect.

If she controls herself after the warning, thank her. If, however, she blows past the warning and continues with the attitude, then follow through with the consequence. That's respectful and fair. She chose to ignore the warning. By choosing the behavior she chose the consequence.

After the consequence has been delivered, she'll potentially push back and fuss, and maybe even call you "the worst parents in the world." DO NOT ENGAGE. Keep it neutral and she'll quickly see that she can no longer push your buttons.

She's bright so she will very quickly catch on to the fact that the rules of the game have changed at home and she will no longer get away with treating her parents disrespectfully. Hopefully, harmony will return to your home and family.

AA 6.3 "What do you do if your friend is bullying you and you don't want to hurt them?" Sounds like you're getting hurt by a friend but aren't willing to stand up for yourself. You may think your silence will make things more peaceful in the friendship. It won't. When you keep quiet the message to your friend is: "I have no problem with the way you're treating me. Keep right on doing what you're doing." I know that's not what you want to communicate otherwise you wouldn't have asked me this question. I care about you, and that's why I want you to learn to be your own best friend.

That means sending a different message—one that reads, "I deserve to be treated with respect." This new self-respecting message won't guarantee respect from others, but it does mean that when people treat you badly, you let them know it's not OK.

You say you're being hurt but you don't want to "hurt" your friend by telling him/her to cut it out. I understand your hesitation. Nobody likes to be told that they're out of line. Your friend might get mad at you, and that's never pleasant. S/he might say, "I don't know what you're talking about." In which case you're left feeling confused and embarrassed. Your friend might even accuse you of trying to "ruin" the friendship and may turn other friends against you. OR . . . s/he might stop and think about what you've just said and make some positive changes. That would be a good thing, right? But when we stay silent about things that are bothering us, the person who is "bullying" continues to bully. Things usually just stay the same or get worse. But when we're brave enough to risk standing up for ourselves (or for others who are being mistreated) we open the door for change.

AA 6.4 "My boyfriend broke up with me online because he says we never really connected." I understand why you find this form of communication frustrating. When we have something important to talk about with a parent, a friend, a bf/gf, or another important person, it really helps to be able to look each other in the eye, read facial expressions, check out body language, and hear the other person's tone of voice. We don't get any of that nonverbal communication when all we do is text and chat. Not talking with you in person, especially when he knew his news would upset you, wasn't very respectful or compassionate. When it comes to healthy relationships (the only kind worth having) it makes sense to choose people who share your values. Because good communication and treating people with respect and compassion is important to you, I suggest you make sure that the next guy you get involved with (trust me, there will be others) knows these things.

As for the fact that you still care, it's natural to feel that longing, but the door seems closed for now. And maybe what you're longing for is a fantasy of the relationship you want, not actually what you had with your ex. Is that possible?

My advice is to let go of this one and open yourself to new friendships. Keep in mind what's important to you, and take what you've learned here and move forward.

CHAPTER 7

AA 7.1 *"My son always acts like he's the victim."* What you describe between the cousins sounds like typical "kid stuff" but your concern that your son "always jumps to feeling like he is the victim" raises a red flag. When your son is at home and/or at school, does he often act as if he is "the victim"?

Round two from Mom—*I see the victim behavior at home and school. He blames his teachers for his missing homework. He blames me for how he is feeling or if he doesn't have clean shorts to wear, even though he is responsible for his own laundry. I try to explain to him about accepting responsibility for his actions/ behavior.*

My reply—Children often imitate the behavior of important adults if they see that adult's behavior as a successful for handling life's "bumps." Would you say that either you or the boy's father are likely to "blame others" for things that may be due to your own actions?

Round three from Mom—*Honestly, my ex-husband constantly blames life's challenges on external causes instead of evaluating his part in the problem/situation. I remember when my son was a young child and he fell against a door and hit his head; his father blamed the door by saying to my son, "Bad door." Recently my son had an issue with a classmate at school and on Facebook, and his dad blamed the girl and her upbringing. I, however, held my son accountable for his actions, and he eventually saw the part he had played in the situation and took responsibility—at least that's what he lead me to believe. I'm not sure if he changed his tune with his dad, who he absolutely idealizes.*

My reply—Part of growing up and becoming a mature adult is learning to take responsibility for your own actions (and the consequences of those actions). Your son is 12, and he's got a lot of maturing to do. I'm sure he will figure things out, in part, on his own and in part with the help of compassionate feedback from you and other people he respects. Yes, it's challenging when the two most important people in his life are not on the same page about taking responsibility, but as he goes through middle and high school, he will continue to have other powerful "influencers" amongst his peers. From them he's likely to get called out for his tendency to blame others and shy away from responsibility for his own actions. Hopefully he will adjust his attitude so that he can develop the level of self-awareness he needs to create and maintain healthy relationships.

AA 7.2 *"My mom always gets mad at me because of my attitude!"* I am listening and I understand what you're saying . . . totally. You want to feel like your mom notices what a unique and interesting person you are. You want to know that you are special to her. You see the way she treats your sister, and it feels unfair to you. That your sister gets "special" treatment and is praised for what she does where it seems to you that whatever you do is not good enough to get your mom's highest praise.

This is a tough situation. I'm sure your mom loves you (you know that's true) but, as you say, "sometimes she has a funny way of showing it." I wonder if the two of you have recently gotten into a pattern where it's become a habit to find fault with each other and to be crabby. Maybe if your mom were aware of how you've been feeling, she'd make more of an effort to be more patient with you and to show you that she loves you and your sister equally. Maybe if the two of you talked about this—calmly and respectfully with you taking the lead—you would be learn something about each other, and figure out a new way of being in this relationship.

I'm so glad to hear that you and your dad have such a healthy relationship. That's wonderful! What do you think of the idea of talking to him about what's going on with you and Mom? I think he could be a very powerful ally in this situation. After all, he loves you both, and surely he's noticed that the relationship needs more peace and understanding.

Think you could talk to your dad about all this and ask for his help?

Round two from 13-year-old—*Thanks, that helped a lot. I might feel a little uncomfortable talking to my dad about it. I don't know why, but I usually keep to myself around my dad. So I guess I'll try and handle this myself. :)*

My reply—Either way, I'm guessing your mom doesn't really know how you feel. Since you're such a good writer, maybe you could write her a "letter" (that you hand to her) expressing to her what you expressed to me. Just a thought.

AA 7.3 *"Am I overreacting to my daughter's makeup and clothing choices?"* It sounds as if you don't believe you have any power over what your 12-year-old does. You actually have all the power you need. I'm just wondering why you haven't been asserting yourself since you feel so strongly about this issue. It seems as if there is a piece missing from this story.

Were you with her when she shopped for the clothes you object to and did you pay for them? By doing that you sent your daughter the message that what she picked out was OK with you. If you didn't approve of her clothing choices then you shouldn't have paid for them.

Round two from Mom—*My husband bought most of the clothes. When I have gone with her she tries them on in the dressing room, and I don't realize that they are off the shoulder type shirts that I'm just uncomfortable with. She has also purchased some of the clothes with her own money. I do feel a bit powerless—my husband and my son seemed to feel I was overreacting but she has one friend whose parents are telling their daughter that my daughter is not a good influence. I've tried to explain to her that people will make impressions based on how you look. I think my husband is starting to understand the implications of letting her dress provocatively and wear makeup.*

My reply—Your daughter needs you to be a leader because she doesn't yet understand the social consequences of her "provocative" clothing choices. When she dresses like this she sends a clear message to the boys at school. (You don't need me to spell out what that message is!) She is also making herself unacceptable to some of the other girls, who will make assumptions about her and call her names. You and your husband need to be a united front. Educate him so that both of you are telling your daughter the same thing: "It is not acceptable for you to dress like this. You are our daughter, and these are the rules in this family." Please tell your 18-year-old son you'd appreciate his butting out on this one.

AA 7.4 *"Why don't I have any luck in guy-hunting?"* I understand why you feel left out when all your friends have boyfriends and you've never had one. Meeting someone and just "clicking" is partly just random luck. While you can't do anything about the "luck factor" you certainly can do something about your attitude. Go around thinking "I'm sick of my relationship life sucking!" and people (guys) will pick up on the fact that you feel sorry for yourself—and also feel a little desperate. You say, "I feel like I'm doomed to be alone forever." Walking around with that assumption is also not likely to attract anyone to you.

Take your own advice when you say, "I realize it's dumb to feel the need to be validated by being in a relationship." That's 100 percent true. You wrote it but you don't believe it. Here's what I can add: Take a vacation from this attitude that not having a boyfriend is a "problem." It's not a problem, though for a while now you have decided that it is. How about if a smart girl like you makes a different decision? For the next two weeks, how about deciding that not having a boyfriend is a good thing? See where that takes you.

CHAPTER 8

AA 8.1 *"My two best friends complain about not having more friends, but they're so judgmental of everyone!"* I can certainly understand why you don't like being around negativity. Hanging out with these "judgmental" friends seems to be bringing you down so you'd rather spend time with more positive people. And of course, you have the right to do that, but you don't want to hurt your best friends' feelings by spending less time with them. It makes you uncomfortable to be with these friends while they're putting others down, and it also makes you uncomfortable to walk away from them. Dealing with friendship issues can be very complicated!

When people are super judgmental, like your two friends, it often means that they're not super-confident about themselves. Instead of trying to make more friends, they stay in their little huddle, just the two of them, and put down everyone else. My guess is that they are afraid to make new friends. Other people stay away from them because no one expects to be judged by a real friend.

You say you feel "stuck" in this situation, but honestly, we are only as stuck as we let ourselves be. You always have options for moving forward.

1. Talk to your friends about how it makes you feel being with them when they're putting down other people. Tell them that you are no longer going to hang around listening to them complaining because it's more fun being with them when they're not complaining.

2. If their behavior doesn't change, then take a vacation from this friendship—a break to spend time with other friends.

3. Being a good friend means, being a good friend to yourself *first*. When friends consistently behave in a way that makes you uncomfortable, you're not doing yourself or the friendship any favors by sticking around and letting it continue.

AA 8.2 "My friend is being bullied but he doesn't want me to tell anyone." I'm really sorry that your friend is going through this. That is so unfair! You know what else is unfair? That the bullies are getting away with it. I think it would help to get adults involved. I know that sometimes students tell teachers and counselors what's going on and nothing changes. That's wrong and totally unfair as well! Adults need to listen to kids and to help them whenever they can.

I don't know what kind of school your friend goes to but maybe it's the kind where teachers, assistant principals, counselors, and other staff members really do care. He needs to tell an adult.

By the way, do his parents know this is going on? If not, they definitely need to know. How can they help their son if they don't know he needs help?

He may have told you he doesn't want your help (and I understand his fear), but he DOES want this to stop. That's why he confided in you. Please tell him that he needs to speak up. If he stays silent this will only continue. If he says "no way" then try to convince him. If you can't convince him to speak up, then offer to go with him to the school counselor or principal. If he refuses, then tell him, "I am your friend, and I will not stand by and let you get bullied any more. If you do not let me come with you to talk with the principal about this, I have to go on my own. Because I care about you."

AA 8.3 "My daughter is being a mean girl to her friend." You sound like a very tuned-in parent. Your family is going through a huge transition, and you don't need me to tell you this is hard on everyone in the family (and will continue to be so) for a while. You are the leader of your family. You are also your 13-year-old daughter's mentor when it comes to her learning how to respond to life's adversities . . . especially in the area of "being hurt by people you trusted." Because you have pointed out the connection between her emotional state and the divorce, I have to ask you, how are you doing through all of this?

What have you said to your daughter about how you're feeling? Obviously you don't want to trash her father, but neither is it helpful for you to "put on a happy face" when you are feeling hurt and angry and betrayed. We want to teach our kids to express intense emotions in appropriate and responsible ways. I agree, it's likely that your daughter is very upset about the divorce . . . probably for many reasons. If (to your knowledge) she didn't exhibit "mean girl" behavior in the past, there is a likely connection between her "meanness" and her feelings about what's going on in the family. I also agree that should never be an excuse to treat people disrespectfully.

You need to talk with her. Choose a quiet time where you won't have any interruptions (turn off the phones), and tell her about the call from her friend's mom. Your tone should be neutral (vs. accusing). For example, "Mary's mom called and told me Mary's upset by some things you've done and said. I'd like to know what's going on." Then close your mouth and listen. See where it goes from there.

Your goal is to get your daughter to trust you with some of the emotions she's feeling, so it's very important that you listen much more than you talk. Be supportive. Be kind. Be encouraging. You may create an important opportunity for your daughter to get real with you . . . about the divorce . . . about her feelings, and ultimately, about the choices she's making (with Mary) that are unnecessarily cruel.

Be very clear with her that she can come to you whenever she feels upset or confused about any "social garbage" going on at school. Tell her that YOU know she is not a mean girl, but that if she treats people rudely, she may convince others that she is. While we all feel angry from time to time —angry enough to want to hurt other people's feelings to get back at them—it is never OK to be cruel or mean or disrespectful. She's a better person than that. So . . . in the future, whenever she is angry, she is to calm herself down (slow deep breaths work!) and stop and think about what she is about to do. "Is this mean? Am I really the kind of person who starts rumors, lies, and says hurtful things? Or am I someone who can deal with my feelings in responsible ways?" What are some responsible ways of dealing with intense feelings? You need to educate her in this area.

AA 8.4 "I don't have friends at my new school, and my old friends have forgotten me." It's can be a real challenge to find your place in a new school. I can understand why you're feeling upset. Things have changed in your life. You didn't choose these changes, but they are part of what's happening here and now. You can feel sorry for yourself or get angry with your old friends. You can blame your parents for the move that has put you in this situation, but none of that will help you make new friends and find your way in your school.

But this might: Right now, here, at the computer, sit up a bit straighter. Take your hands off the keyboard and rest them *lightly* on the top of your legs. Close your eyes and inhale . . . *slowly* . . . through your nose. Then relax your jaw, open your mouth and exhale . . . *slowly*. Repeat. Notice your breath coming in and going out. Keep breathing in this slow, calm way. This is called a re-centering breath and it should help you calm down and feel better.

Now here's my advice: Talk to your old friends. Without whining, or complaining, or trying to turn them against the new girl. Talk to them about getting together over the holiday break (if possible). Hopefully that will make you feel better. Another thing that might make you feel better is to remember that you are a great friend. Maybe the reason you don't have any new friends yet is because the kids at your new school don't know you. So tomorrow at school, be friendly. Smile. Say hi to people. That's how most friendships begin. You're in a new world and this is a new beginning. Go for it!

QT: QUIZZES AND EMPOWERMENT TOOLS

CHAPTER 2

QT 2.1 A Family Meeting Plan

Family meetings offer great opportunities for you and your kids to connect more deeply, to become better listeners, to learn the art of compromise, and to validate your collective ability to work together effectively and compassionately to resolve problems.

Step #1: Schedule the Meeting. Pick a time that works for everyone. As a family you can decide to hold regularly scheduled meetings. In addition, anyone in the family should have the right to call a family meeting at any time.

Step #2: Create Ground Rules, Take Turns Talking. To highlight respect for the person who is speaking, your family may choose to pass an object of some sort—also known as the *talking stick*. The current speaker holds on to it until s/he is finished. If anyone interrupts, the speaker can calmly say, "Excuse me, but I have the talking stick." When our own kids were younger, we used a wooden spoon for this purpose. Now that they're adults, we can easily talk and listen to each other. (See how good habits take hold?)

Step #3: Talking and Listening. Listen attentively without interrupting. Same goes for invalidating or contradicting the speaker. A family meeting needs to be a safe place to talk about feelings. That can only happen when we really listen. This helps build trust in all directions.

Stick to the topic at hand. Don't bring up past problems. It only adds to the emotion and the need to defend oneself. It also undermines the feeling of safety and does nothing to help resolve the current conflict. Stay focused in present time.

Stick to your own feelings. Use I-messages. Say things like "I feel _____ when you _____." As in: "I feel frustrated when you don't do your chores" or "I feel worried when you and dad yell at each other." When each speaker focuses on his/her own feelings, listeners are less likely to feel attacked because no one's blaming them for anything. Speaking of blame: Avoid words like "You always . . ." or "You never . . ." during meetings. When you start accusing and putting people down, they usually stop listening and counterattack. This never helps resolve problems and has no place in a family meeting. (Or any healthy relationship for that matter.)

Some families only call family meetings when there's a major issue to discuss. Other families like to hold meetings

238

on a regular basis to "clear the air" and give everyone a chance to speak their mind. Still other families have a tradition of a "go around" at the dinner table, where everyone weighs in on the challenges and successes of the day. It doesn't really matter how or when your family gets together to talk—the important thing is that you communicate openly and share your feelings, listening to what others have to say, and working together to resolve problems together as a family.

QT 2.2 QUIZ—*Family Climate Questionnaire*

On a scale of 1–5, how true is each statement?
1=Never True
2=Almost Never True
3=Sometimes True
4=Almost Always True
5=Always True

NOTE: This questionnaire assesses what's true for you and your child right now about your experience of being part of your family. There are no right or wrong answers.

I feel respected in my family.
1   2   3   4   5
People in my family are kind to one another.
1   2   3   4   5
People in my family understand me.
1   2   3   4   5
I pretend things are OK when they're not.
1   2   3   4   5
I tell people how I really feel.
1   2   3   4   5
In our family we have fun.
1   2   3   4   5

TEACHING KIDS TO BE GOOD PEOPLE

I sometimes do/say things I regret.

1   2   3   4   5

After we get angry, we apologize and talk things through.

1   2   3   4   5

I wish we had a closer family.

1   2   3   4   5

We help each other.

1   2   3   4   5

QT 2.3 QUIZ—How Much of a Sheeple Am I? True or False?

1. If someone thinks something's funny, I laugh even if I don't get the joke. T or F

2. If everyone is talking about a movie I haven't seen, I'll pretend I saw it. T or F

3. If people are teasing someone, I will do it to, even if that person never did anything to me. T or F

4. I try really hard not to make a fool of myself. T or F

5. I'd do anything to be more popular. T or F

6. I've quit an activity I liked because my friends weren't into it. T or F

7. I worry about people talking behind my back. T or F

8. If someone makes a rude comment about something I'm wearing, I won't wear it again. T or F

9. I have bought things just to impress other people. T or F

240

10. I have publicly changed my opinion because no one agreed with me. T or F

If you got:

7–10 Ts: You have some strong sheepish tendencies that can prevent you from calling your own shots. You might want to cut loose from the herd every now and then, just to prove to yourself that you are still an individual. You are, aren't you?

4–6 Ts: You sometimes find it challenging to stand up for yourself so you don't push it very often. But sometimes you are your own person, and it actually feels good.

0–3 Ts: Most of the time you don't hesitate to think for yourself. Your friends might respect you for being independent and whether you know it or not, you could be inspiring others to think for themselves, too.

CHAPTER 3

QT 3.1 Getting Unstuck with Your Next Best Move

When we're upset we usually don't think very clearly. It's hard to see the Bigger Picture. Good chance we'll say and/or do something we'll later regret. Help your child (and yourself) calm down and think things through with this nine-step strategy. If your child is willing to talk about what's going on, these steps can help you help your son/daughter to figure out the next best move. Not ready to talk yet? Respect that and check back in a while. If your child is unwilling to talk to you for whatever reason and your gut says s/he needs to talk to someone . . . get the help of another trusted adult.

Step #1: Tell the Truth. Encourage your child to acknowledge that s/he is upset. It's a positive first step for us to say, "I'm STRESSED!" That's much healthier and more productive than pretending we're OK when we're not.

Step #2: Stop. Put on the brakes. Even if you're in the middle of something important, taking a break is *more* important. Proceeding while stressed is likely to a) contribute to thoughtless mistakes and/or b) make the situation worse.

Step #3: Calm Down. Tell your child (calmly and firmly) to calm down. Suggest some re-centering breaths. (Inhale slowly and evenly through your nose, then relax your jaw, open your mouth and exhale slowly and evenly. Repeat three to five times. It will relax you.) Not into relaxation breathing? Whatever it takes to calm down is good as long as it's legal and healthy. If your child asks, "Why should I calm down?" you can answer: "Because it's the best thing you can do right now for yourself and the people around you." Explain that if s/he doesn't calm down, stress will take control, and solving the problem will be more difficult.

Step #4: Fuel for Thought. Encourage your child to ask: "What am I trying to accomplish in this situation?" In other words: "What's your goal?"

Step #5: Think Some More. Referring to what your child said in #4, ask: "Can you personally make that happen?" If the goal requires a change in someone else's feelings or behavior, then that goal is beyond his/her control. In that case, s/he has to let it go. Help reframe the goal so that what your child is aiming for is actually influenced by his/her own choices. That's all anyone ever can control.

Step #6: Explore Options. Ask: What are your *options* for reaching your goal? Help your child make a list of all available options, and predict what might reasonably happen in each instance. Even young children can learn to do this when they're calm. Don't evaluate options for them. Remain neutral. This is an exercise in critical thinking. Your job is to facilitate the process. Let your child think things through and come to his/her own conclusions.

Step #7: Choose the Best Option. That would be the one that best reflects respect and compassion. Options which intentionally hurt or humiliate others, seek revenge, or put anyone at risk are unacceptable. Teach your child that no matter how angry or hurt you may be feeling, *cruel's not cool!* Cruelty is a form of violence. It's wrong. It will make the situation worse and bring you back to #1.

Step #8: Take Action. Encourage your child to act on the option that makes most sense for the greater good.

Step #9: Kudos. Acknowledge your child for calming down, thinking things through, and doing the right thing.

QT 3.2 QUIZ—Assumption or Fact?

1. "My child(ren) will always need my help." A or F

2. "I always know what's best for my kid." A or F

3. "I'll do it for them and eventually they'll learn to do it for themselves." A or F

4. "Doing everything for them is my job!" A or F

5. "If they don't need me as much, then they won't love me as much." A or F

6. "A good parent always does as much as possible for a child." A or F

7. "If I am too strict they'll hate me." A or F

8. "Children of stay-at-home parents are less independent than those of working parents." A or F

9. "The way my parents raised me will work just fine for my kids." A or F

10. "Parents who push their kids toward independence don't really enjoy being parents." A or F

Answers: These are all assumptions. If you thought any of them were facts, have a look at the Assumptions Toolkit (QT 3.3). It can help you deconstruct assumptions so that you can see more clearly and teach more effectively.

QT 3.3 Parents Helping Kids: Assumptions Toolkit

Unreasonable assumptions can keep us from understanding the truth about our teaching role as parents:

1. **Name one of your parenting assumptions.** For example, let's take #6 from the above quiz: "A good parent always does as much as possible for a child."

2. **Ask yourself:**
   A. **Where did that assumption come from?** We're not born with any assumptions, especially not ones about

parenting. All of our assumptions come from somewhere. Figuring out the source of our assumptions can help us examine them more objectively. Sample answer: "My parents were great parents and they always did everything for me."

B. **How does that assumption help me?** My theory is that we hang on to assumptions that help us in some way, comfort us, massage our egos, and make us feel like we belong. Sample answer: "Everyone thinks I'm a great parent. I like that."

C. **What problem has that assumption caused?** When it comes to unreasonable assumptions, there is often a price to pay for clinging to them. Sample answer: "Sometimes I feel like everything I do is for the kids and it's too much. When I feel I have no time for myself, I resent them and their demands. Then I feel guilty for feeling that way."

D. **How might things be different for you and your family, if that assumption was wrong?** Sample answer: "If I could be a good parent without always doing everything, I'd feel freer and less resentful. And my kids might become more mature and independent."

3. **Still want to hold on to that assumption?** Because it is your choice to hang on to it or not. Sample answer: "Uh . . . I'll get back to you right after I type my son's term paper and finish my daughter's science project! (Just kidding!)"

CHAPTER 6

QT 6.1 A Parent's Pledge to Raise a Responsible Digital Citizen

About three-quarters of young people ages 12–17 regularly use social media. The Pew Research Center has found that 88 percent of them say they've seen someone being mean or cruel to another person on a social networking site. While our tweens and teens are scary good at navigating technology, when it comes to connecting the dots between their digital choices and the resulting social consequences, most are clueless. If your child has a cellphone and Internet access then it's up to you to teach him/her how to behave.

Q: If you don't, who will?
A: Their equally clueless friends.

Social media is part of the lives of our 21st century kids. Consider taking this pledge to raise a responsible young Net citizen by teaching your children appropriate online behavior. I pledge:

☞ to support my child's use of age-appropriate social networking sites and to teach my child how to play safe and stay safe online so s/he can grow in positive ways from online activities.

☞ to teach my child the difference between what is and what is not responsible and appropriate online behavior. That includes teaching my child the best ways to respond to anything online that makes him/her uncomfortable, angry, or scared.

☞ to help my child understand the risks of giving out or posting personal information publicly online (including photos, age, last name, name of school, home address, phone number).

☞ to keep in mind the fact that digitally savvy kids have "status anxiety" (a need to be accepted) which directly affects their online behavior. My child has the right to choose his/her friends, but not the right to demean, harass, or intimidate others. I pledge to make sure s/he gets this message and acts accordingly.

☞ to have open, respectful dialogues with my child about how s/he uses the online services I provide access to. When my child messes up (it'll happen), I pledge to use the opportunity to teach him/her more socially acceptable behavior.

☞ to help my child discern between a true friend and someone with bad intentions, so that s/he can use good judgment regarding online "friends," as well as his/her own behavior.

☞ to educate my child on how their public online activity leaves a lasting digital footprint that teachers, college admissions officers, or future employers may see.

☞ to help my child understand the implications of online behavior so that my child can maintain his/her privacy, safety, and good reputation while we keep a healthy, trusting, and mutually respectful relationship between us.

You don't need me to tell you why this stuff is important. So . . . can we all count on each other to do this?

CHAPTER 7

QT 7.1 *Improving Parent-Teen Relationships*

Because moods and attitudes can shift on a dime, parents of tweens and teens often face unique challenges. Amidst the typical upheavals of the teen years, you've got to focus on your job description: Raise an independent, fully functioning young adult who consistently makes choices that demonstrate compassion, respect, and social courage.

There's no single golden rulebook for parenting (though the one you're reading is highly recommended). That said, keeping these 10 tips in mind will help you stay centered. And that's exactly where you do your most effective parenting.

Tip #1: Remember that you are the parent. Your job is to protect your child and help him/her to become a good person who does good in the world. Being a leader and a compassionate teacher is more important than being your teen's friend.

Tip #2: Remain calm. Nothing gets resolved when stress and emotions make it impossible to think clearly. If you can't respond rationally and empathetically, then take a break until you can.

Tip #3: Talk less and listen more. Just like the rest of us, teens want to be respected and heard. Be a "safe" and available person to talk to.

Tip #4: Find the balance. A key challenge in parenting is to remain emotionally connected while granting teens increasingly more opportunities to use their own judgment.

Tip #5: Model what you're teaching. Want your teen to be trustworthy, responsible, and compassionate? Make sure you're consistently modeling those values in your own life.

Tip #6: Make your expectations clear and *be consistent* with your follow-through. If teens know the privileges earned for following the rules and consequences for disregarding them, they're more likely to make healthy choices.

Tip #7: Catch your teen in the act of doing something right. Praise shows that you noticed their efforts. It also promotes a feeling of competency.

Tip #8: Be real. Mom/Dad do NOT always know best. Admit your own confusion and mistakes. Apologize when appropriate. Show your kids that just like them, you are also "a work in progress."

Tip #9: Create time to enjoy being a family. Having regular meals together, relaxing, and unplugging from technology is a gift with long-lasting benefits.

Tip #10: *Lighten up!* Humor is a great de-stressor. Remember, no one stays a teen (or the parent of a teen) forever!

CHAPTER 8

QT 8.1 How to Raise Young Adults Who Are at Home with Themselves

☞ **Create a home base that's a safety net and a launching pad.** The home we make for our children needs to support emotional development and nurture the spirit. With a stable, loving, and accepting family to return to, anything is possible . . . even venturing into the unknown. Kids who grow up with a strong foundation are like turtles, always carrying their sense of home along with them. Remind yourself as often as needed that your goal is to prepare your children for life. That means helping them develop critical thinking plus ethical choice making skills. It also means acting with compassion, kindness, and generosity of spirit. Whenever you catch your teens doing or saying something that demonstrates these capacities, let them know you approve. It helps them develop a positive self-image, essential for feeling at home with themselves.

☞ **Uncertainty is not a dirty word.** When you know absolutely what you stand for then you should absolutely take a stand. That's a great message for adolescents who often let their addiction to peer approval steer them away from what they know is right. But uncertainty is part of life. Kids brought up to believe that doubt isn't an acceptable emotion are reluctant to try new things. How can they be at home with themselves if they're unwilling to experience confusion? How can they be at home in the world if they're not open to new things? If you truly want them to become self-confident adults who move through life with grace and courage, then they need occasionally to feel something akin to "I have no idea what to do in this situation!" Sometimes things only become clear after we've had the courage to venture forth armed only with uncertainty and a willingness to accept what crosses our path, take it in, and learn from it. Let them know that it's OK not to know.

☞ **Model adaptability and an open attitude.** If you tend to be anxious about the future, your attitude may be making it all that more difficult for your kids to feel at home anywhere. Ask yourself these questions:

- o   Do you like surprises?

- o   Do you enjoy: Meeting new people? Eating new foods? Listening to new music? Going to places and doing things you've never done before?

- o   Do you take time to notice your surroundings?

- o   Are you critical or suspicious of things that are different?

- o   When you're feeling "out of your element" do you usually: Shut down and withdraw? Become combative and defensive? Have a drink? Crank up the volume of your social self? Acknowledge your discomfort and try to relax and become more open?

If your temperament drives you toward needing to feel in control then challenge yourself to become a bit more flexible. The more open you are to change (planned or otherwise) the more adaptable your kids will be.

☞ **Travel, as a family**. If you're planning a family vacation, you might use this opportunity to step back a bit and let your kids show what they've already learned about being at home in the world. Notice their competencies and acknowledge them for it. And if you're traveling to a new place, you might take the point of view that you are all strangers in a strange land together. As "strangers," your family has a chance to observe, learn, and push the edges of your collective comfort zones. You can talk about that and share your feelings. Yes, being in a strange new place can be scary, but it can also reinforce how strong and capable each of you is.

Even if travel is not an option for you and your family, there are plenty of ways to explore other cultures. Those include: ethnic restaurants, cultural festivals, art exhibits, films, music, books and stories from other cultures and of course, the Internet. Without going very far, you can teach your child about the wider world so that s/he develops an open-minded attitude toward "what's out there."

☞ **Encourage independence.** Each year, your child ought to be stepping up while you step back. For teens, it's nearly time for them to take over as their own manager. They'll need that experience when they actually leave home. They'll also need to know that "home" (including their growing self-confidence, plus your love and everything you've taught them) is always right there in their heart, nurturing their spirit.

ABOUT THE AUTHOR

ANNIE FOX is an internationally respected character educator and the author of five books for teens about growing up and getting along. Her books include *The Teen Survival Guide to Dating and Relating, Too Stressed to Think?* (with Ruth Kirschner), and the popular Middle School Confidential™ book and app series. Since 1997, when she launched groundbreaking teen website The InSite, Annie has been answering teen and parenting questions from around the world. Because of her unique insight into adult-teen relationships, she is a sought-after speaker who takes equal delight connecting with students, educators, and parents.

Annie Fox may be reached through her website, www.AnnieFox.com

15593367R00156

Made in the USA
Charleston, SC
11 November 2012